THE SOUL
OF A
GENERATION

ADDRESSING THE CRISIS OF FAITH
IN TODAY'S YOUTH CULTURE

KEN DORNHECKER

The Soul Of A Generation
Addressing the Crisis of Faith in Today's Youth Culture
by Ken Dornhecker

Printed in the United States of America

ISBN 978-1-60266-729-7

www.xulonpress.com

To

Rick Eubanks
the youth pastor who discipled me
at his kitchen table.

Contents

∾⧲∿

Chapter 1

Multitudes, Multitudes in the Valley of Decision!

I would like to ask you to imagine your church on a typical Sunday morning—all the believers gathering to encourage one another, to worship God, and to hear His Word. Picture in your mind all the genuinely joyful people streaming through the corridors and eventually filling the morning worship service... Now imagine **95%** of the people simply vanishing before your very eyes. What would it be like? Instead of the joyous clamor of loving fellowship, there is now only a pitiful defeated silence in the halls.

In the morning worship service, picture the empty seats. Think of what it would be like for a mere handful of you rattling around in the near empty facility. Next imagine church buildings going up for sale, and then being converted to nightclubs, entertainment complexes, condos, and health clubs. Imagine a completely marginalized church made up primarily of a tiny number of senior citizens exerting almost no influence on culture. Imagine only a small percentage of society even claiming to be Christians.

Most tragic of all, think of multitudes of *never-churched* young people with no moral compass inside, giving themselves completely to every sort of destructive behavior. They are empty souls without spiritual dimension—sexually active by middle school, out of control, often violent, and drinking heavily. Now look into the desolate eyes of a secular society.

I've asked you to use your imagination, but sadly, I don't have to. In 1984 I moved to Western Europe as a young missionary. I remember the first day I walked down a street in the slum of the large German city where I had just moved. A block away from our outreach, spray painted on the wall in big letters were the words, *No Future!* Over the next few days I saw it spray painted everywhere I went. I asked one of the other missionaries who had been there much longer what it meant. He told me, "The teens do that here. It is their philosophy of life—drink, take drugs, party, and have sex because there is no tomorrow—No Future!"

Now after having spent more than two decades ministering on that spiritually desolate continent, I have seen with my own eyes the very things described above. In numerous German cities I have seen parks full of wayward teens, hundreds of them, drinking liquor by the bucket, literally! Twelve and thirteen year old boys and girls sitting around in little circles sucking booze out of buckets with giant straws, the ground around them littered with empty bottles. There are also sporadic outbursts of violence, smashing of public property, and even fits of rage toward each other. Promiscuity naturally abounds in these near orgy conditions. Sadly and shockingly their behavior looks more animal than human, like something out of a nature documentary rather than modern city dwellers in a western society.

In 2005, my wife and I were traveling around Germany preaching in youth camps and in the marketplaces. We were also keeping one eye on the news because of events happening in the neighboring country of France. The French capital, Paris, deteriorated into anarchy as the *juvenile population* exploded into riots. It quickly spread to every large urban area of the entire nation as well as into some rural regions. For several weeks, large unruly mobs of wayward youth simply took over sections of the cities, burning cars, breaking shop windows, and fighting riot police. A state of emergency was declared by President Jacques Chirac. In the end, 126 firefighters and police were injured, one person was killed, nearly three thousand were arrested, 274 towns were affected, 8973 vehicles were torched, and countless buildings were damaged. The damage was estimated at 250 million dollars.[1]

Europe, once a bastion of Christianity, a continent where the sparks of the greatest global revivals and awakenings in history began, has now become the world's most atheistic continent. The lands of Luther, Calvin, Whitefield, and Wesley now lie in spiritual ruin. For decades the huge cathedrals and churches have stood relatively empty, a literal shell of what they once were.

The number of actual worshipers has dwindled away on Sunday mornings to a mere handful in these once vibrant places of worship. They are kept up by governments and donations from the tourists who come to view them. They are now nothing more than dusty old museums, relics of Europe's distant spiritual past. Now even that is changing. Recently I saw an actual news story showing those very cathedrals and churches being *de-sanctified*, permanently closed, and sold off. They are being converted to health clubs, entertainment centers, night clubs, and condos across the UK and Western Europe.[2] In most of Western Europe the evangelical population is less then 1%. In France, atheism represents more than 30% of that society. Europe has become a secular, spiritual wasteland!

What does all this have to do with America's spiritual condition? I am absolutely convinced we are only one generation behind Europe. We will not have to simply imagine much longer this horrible picture taking place here. It is **already** taking place at an alarming rate within the *Millennial Generation* (born 1982 - 2000). Many examples serve to show us the monumental shift occurring within our own culture. When I was a teen, the adage, *boys will be boys* surely applied. There were no shortage of bad boys, but girls were a different story. At least on most levels they could be counted on to behave decently. Apparently, that is no longer the case. "In 1965 a survey of college students showed that 33% of the males and 70% of the females thought premarital sex was wrong, but today the figures are all the way down to 16% and 17%." [3]

Statistics don't always capture the true gravity of a situation though. What is most disturbing is the kinds of activities in which our young people are getting involved. A recent broadcast of *ABC's 20/20*, as well as other current television news magazine programs, have documented several alarming new trends in youth behavior. The combination of digital photography, and the *wild west* internet culture our teens are so enamored with, is spawning a truly undreamed of tangle of serious sin. Teenage girls desperately seeking notoriety and attention are producing provocative homemade porn and uploading it to the internet for all to see. [4]

I'll never forget the shock and sadness on a crushed father's face as a television host showed him his sixteen year old daughter's blog-page featuring pornographic nude photos of her. Other girls, as well as boys, film themselves committing random acts of brutal violence against other teens and post it on the enormously popular internet video sites. And these are not isolated incidences, but daily occurrences in the current internet youth culture. [5]

This *bad behavior* is real and is producing serious consequences within our society, not to mention the devastation it is visiting upon the lives of the young people involved. One example, the number of girls under sixteen committing serious crimes involving violence, like assault, has doubled in the last ten years. My point is not to pick on the girls because certainly no case could be made for boys improving their behavior in the last decade either. It is undeniable that a dangerous slide has begun in our youth culture.

In 2003, I began to spend a great deal of time on college campuses dialoging with the students. What is most troubling to me is the young people I encounter today at America's universities are buying wholesale into the exact same belief system of the youth culture I witnessed in Europe in 1984.

To say we are literally engaged in a life and death struggle for the very soul of a generation may sound overly dramatic, but the purpose of this message is to alert us to the reality that we really are in such an urgent and desperate struggle.

A most alarming development came to light as I researched this book. Reading the latest materials regarding the spiritual trends on this generation, something astounding kept emerging. Over and over, I kept coming to the unmistakable conclusion that **two-thirds** of the kids raised in church by Christian parents are rejecting that faith. In category after category, within a couple of points of sixty-six percent **(66%)**, they are discarding the message of the New Testament.

∞ They do **NOT** believe Jesus is the Son of God.
∞ They do **NOT** plan to make church a part of their lives once they leave home.
∞ They do not believe premarital sex is wrong.
∞ They do not believe the Holy Spirit is real.
∞ They do not believe in moral absolutes.

So rather than constantly overwhelm you with numbers and statistics, I will most often simply refer to this sad **two-thirds** reality. We must grasp the unpleasant and shocking truth that the vast majority of church kids are throwing away faith in Jesus. At least one notable Christian leader, Josh McDowell, has called this possibly *The Last Christian Generation*. For a detailed picture of the statistical reality of the Millennial Generation, see Josh's book by that title.[6]

If we were to ask most parents, *What are your goals for your children?* they would answer, *I want them to have a better life than I had. I want them to get a good education, then get a good job with a comfortable income, get married, and have a nice family of their own someday.* All worthy goals, but what about beyond that? I would hope your ultimate desire for them would be to serve the Lord Jesus Christ on earth and spend eternity with Him in heaven. *Oh yes, that too, of course!* That last one is naturally the most important and perhaps the one we take **most** for granted. We just assume that they will wind up in heaven.

Beating the Odds

The fact is, unless we take action, current trends would suggest the odds are greatly **against** most of this generation going to heaven. I know that statement seems audacious, even irresponsible, but I have solid Biblical grounds for that assessment. In case I'm being too vague, this stat should terrify us. As we've just seen, sixty-three percent **(63%)** of kids raised in church today **do not even** believe Jesus is the Son of the one true God![7] Jesus himself stated in the clearest possible terms what this means. *If you do not believe that I am the one I claim to be, you will indeed die in your sins (John 8:24b).* We must come to grips with how serious this is. To **NOT** believe Jesus is the Son of God means that these young people will lose their souls!

So far I have focused on the rather dismal picture of what kids raised in church believe. What about the millions who have almost no background whatsoever in the Christian faith? If this is what is going on in the church, then how bleak is the picture for those outside? *Multitudes, multitudes in the valley of decision! For the day of the Lord is near in the valley of decision (Joel 3:14).*

That is what this book is all about, the very real possibility of a generation of young people at risk of losing their souls. We are not talking in abstract terms or about a mass of nameless faceless statistics, but rather your kids, your grandchildren, your church's youth group, losing their souls. It is not about stats, it is about young people, multitudes of them, even the majority of those who have been raised in Christian homes, who are throwing away belief in Jesus.

It breaks my heart because they are carelessly discarding the magnificent Son of the Living God, who loves them so much that He died a brutal death on a wooden cross to save their eternal souls. They are recklessly casting aside the only means of salvation that God will ever send their way. Most of them have no idea of the consequences of such a course of action because they have never been warned.

As difficult as it may be, we must face this sobering reality. We dare not think this cannot happen. Jesus himself indicated it can. *What good is it for a man to gain the whole world, yet forfeit his soul? Or what can a man give in exchange for his soul? If anyone is ashamed of me and my words in this adulterous and sinful generation, the Son of Man will be ashamed of him when he comes in his Father's glory with the holy angels (Mark 8:36-38 Emphasis added).* Here Jesus spoke specifically about people losing their very souls—making a poor exchange for their eternal destiny. Furthermore, He seems to indicate that spiritual decay can spread into an entire generation, putting them in real peril. I am fully persuaded that almost an entire generation is losing their soul right before our very eyes.

Chapter 2

Finding a Lost Sense of Urgency

Petra, a great contemporary Christian singing group, had a song in the eighties about a desperate young girl named Annie.*

No one ever noticed Annie weeping.
People all around, but she was all alone.
Mama's got her meetings, Daddy's got his job.
And no one's got the time, so Annie's on her own.
No one ever knew her desperation.
People couldn't hear her cry out silently.
Locked inside the bathroom, she grabs a jar of pills
The medicine that cures becomes the poison that kills.

And it's too late for Annie
She's gone away for good.
There's so much we could tell her,
And now we wish we could...
But it's too late... for Annie

*© Dawn Treader Music All Rights Reserved. Used By Permission

If only we had known her situation
We'd have tried to stop this useless tragedy.
Annie's lost forever, never to be found.
But there are lots of others like her all around.

And it's not too late for Annie, she could be next to you.
Don't miss the chance to tell her before her life is through.
We gotta tell her Jesus loves her
Tell her Jesus cares.
Tell her He can free her and her burdens bear...

It's not too late.

Making a Difference in the Annie Generation!

For me this has become the *Annie generation!* Even though they're not all committing suicide, I perceive them to be in grave danger. There is so much we should tell them before it's too late, before they are lost forever. How can we be successful at telling them things they need to hear before it's too late? How can we actually turn this generation around?

If you look at successful people, the kind of people who make a real impact on the world, you always find someone who is passionate! Whether it is a business owner, a sports figure, or a celebrity, they pour ALL of themselves into their task. People naturally gravitate to that kind of passion and energy. Sometimes these people are not even all that likable, but their raw energy and enthusiasm move others to action! They are people of influence.

To make a difference in this generation of young people, I believe we are going to have to capture and maintain a real sense of urgency. I truly believe that is the overwhelming KEY to unlock this group of kids. As we shall see later, they are drawn to authentic passion. It reaches them!!! That is why we must take the time to get fully persuaded!

Near the one year anniversary of the 9/11 attacks, my wife and I were traveling. At our hotel, our continental breakfast came with a copy of *USA Today*. The cover story featured a huge picture of the World Trade Center towers ablaze, next to a headline that read *Delay Meant Death on 9/11*. In the year following the devastating attack, the newspaper had done an exhaustive study of exactly what had gone on in the towers immediately after the first plane struck the north tower. They interviewed hundreds of people who had walked out of the doomed buildings and studied the records from the New York police and fire departments. They came to four conclusions why some died and some lived. As I read the second conclusion my heart was totally gripped. *People lived and died in groups, influenced to stay or go by those around them.*[1]

From the interviews they determined that from the moment the first plane hit the first tower, people all over both buildings were aware that some terrible event was taking place. But they were confused as to the exact nature of what was happening, or more specifically, how they should react. Most were more or less paralyzed with inaction. At that moment, someone would enter into an office of just such people and immediately begin to say, "We need to leave — to evacuate! Come on right now!" Everyone would respond and head toward the stairs and to safety. Wonderfully, everyone in that office would live!

However, in an office literally right across the hall from the first group, the same confusion and inaction would be taking place simultaneously. But into this office someone would enter with a different message. "Everyone stay calm. Everything is all right. Go back to your desks, sit back down." This group would comply and nervously return to their desks to wait and see what would happen. With very few exceptions these people all died in the tragic events of that day. ***People lived and died in groups, influenced to stay or go by those around them.***

With that thought in mind, I am convinced that we true believers in Jesus Christ must be the voice of influence to this generation—the voice that says *this sin-infected world is not safe. Come with me to the safety of Jesus Christ.* We must rightly perceive the spiritual danger of the times and do all we can to influence the young people we know to flee the devastating consequences that will surely come to this world. We must lead them out of harm's way to the Savior! This is exactly what Jesus has called us to be, people of influence. He said we were to be the *light of the world* and the *salt of the earth.*[2] Salt is a preservative, and we, God's people, must realize we are the preserving factor in a decaying world.

Desperately Crying Out For Someone to Show Them the Way

There used to be a popular saying, *I'm OK, You're OK.*[3] We may not realize it, but this *I'm OK, You're OK* factor has an enormous impact on people all around us. Even if they do not outwardly admit it, people tend to look for the approval of those around them. In other words, they gauge to a large degree how *they* are doing by the affirmation they receive from those closest to them. Particularly, you parents have a real impact on your kids in this way.

Although it may seem that MTV, pop culture, or their friends are molding them, the truth, as overwhelmingly indicated by surveys, is that their greatest source of influence is their parents. I think we also tend to underestimate the tremendous impact a strong spiritual leader can have on an adolescent. Pastors and youth leaders who show a genuine concern for the kids they minister to can have an enormous strategic influence on a kid at just the right time in his or her life. So if the *I'm OK, You're OK* effect is going on, and they are on the wrong road, they need to sense from us a very definite concern. If they do not see any alarm in you, they will take that as affirmation that they are OK.

The power of parental or adult assurance is mind-boggling. I once saw a whole package of clips on a popular video show that demonstrated this. A rapid succession of clips showed young children taking a tumble from a bike or falling down. The moment they came into contact with the ground, their faces instantly contorted into a blend of shock, confusion, pain, and tears! But the common denominator for all the clips was a parent running into frame, scooping the child up, and showering them rapid fire with the single phrase, *You're OK, You're OK, You're OK!* The effect was amazing—almost instantaneous calm, comfort, and reassurance. It is instinctive for a child to reach out for an adult appraisal of their situation.

As a child, I reacted to circumstances completely based on my parent's demeanor. If I felt uneasy about a situation, I glanced at their faces. I could instantly read if everything was OK or not. If I saw so much of a hint of concern on their face, I sensed real danger and generally made an instinctive bee-line for their protection and leadership. They intuitively knew what to do.

If I was obliviously playing in a park and my parents were ready to leave, I could tune them out for several minutes. I would eventually respond to their calls, but not until I had to. However, if completely unbeknownst to me, some danger encroached, my mother or father could summon my full attention in a nano-second simply by the tone of their voice. I would look up and run into the safety of their arms, just as a strange person or danger approached.

There was an unusual edge in their voice that broke through my inattention. I believe when those of us who speak publicly to this generation of young people do so, they need to hear something in our voice that alerts them to the dangers at hand. When we pray for them, we need to pray with a sense of urgency, like their very lives depended on it or their souls were truly at stake.

We must realize most of this generation has no capacity to sense the spiritual danger that surrounds them. If they do **not** see a passion in our eyes, hear concern in our voices, or sense an alarm in our demeanor as they drift away from God and the safety of His Kingdom, they will take that to mean *all is well.* The landmines in a sinful pop culture will inflict horrible wounds on their souls. The subtle devilish doubts and lies about who Jesus really is will crush their trust and faith. Falsely reassured by the *I'm OK, You're OK* effect, they will drift further and further toward destruction. BUT THE TRUTH IS, THEY ARE NOT OK SPIRITUALLY! If they are on what Jesus described as *the broad road that leads to destruction*[4] and they see us acting *business as usual,* they will never perceive that they are in spiritual danger.

Although we may not always realize it, they are probing us, seeking approval or disapproval. They want to see how far they can go before falling off the edge. I often notice as I minister on campuses, students who seem to be purposefully trying to get under my skin are really only fishing for reaction. I have learned how to deflect what seems like a negative at that moment, because I know the real interaction is to come. Secretly, they are desperately crying out for someone to show them the way in this terrifying, morally mixed-up society. Sometimes they tell me that exact thing privately after we have spoken a while. They seem confident, self assured outwardly, but inwardly they are desperately lost in the storm. They are crying out for some adult to be a voice of influence and help them find something solid and real.

The task of making a difference spiritually takes real effort and sometimes we can become weary. Let's face it, ordinary life can often seem like an uphill battle with just the routine struggles we all face. When you add to that the pressure of being a spiritual force for change in the lives of those around you, it takes perseverance. It is just too easy to drift along with the flow rather than exert the effort it takes to influence others toward spiritual good.

In the case of teenagers, it can be especially daunting. They can sometimes send mixed signals about how much they want your advice. So if you do not have a real passion, you might just take the easy road. If you are not fully persuaded of their desperate need, you will probably not fervently pray your heart out for your kids. You will never likely speak earnestly with them about the very real dangers and issues they face until you come to grips with how much is really at stake. Until you find the passion of God, you will not make a real difference! My hope is God will awaken in you a sense of urgency. My prayer is you will find an authentic passion as well as the tools to spiritually impact the lives of young people all around you.

Chapter 3

What They Really Think

I had spoken under a beautiful stand of pine trees the last two afternoons on the attractive campus of the *University of North Carolina at Wilmington*. There had been some lively interaction this second day and I had just wrapped up my open-air preaching for the day. I walked over to the platform under the clock tower where my wife Becky had been sitting. The students sitting here had also heard my preaching. I was ready to call it a day, but just as I reached the platform a young man called out to me, "Hey, come here. Sit down; I want to talk about these things." So I sat down beside him and introduced myself.

Tim started out with quite a chip on his shoulder and was very cocky and arrogant. He told me early on that he had grown up going to church every Sunday of his life. So he was sure there was not much of anything I could tell him about God or the Bible that he did not already know.

Then he *really* said what was on his mind. "I know all about Jesus and the cross and all that, but I don't really want to have anything to do with Him. I just want to live the way I want to live right now. I don't care if it is sinful or if God approves. Right now I'm at college so I'm going to go party and get drunk every weekend. I'm going to have sex with all the girls I can. I don't think God will condemn me for that. I mean the whole format of church is just not right—this old pastor guy standing up there, trying to teach me and tell me how to live. **I mean young people from my generation, we don't like to be told what to do.** Why should we listen?"

I started with his last objection about *church* being all wrong. "Well," I asked, "do you go to class here?"

"Yes, of course."

"Are some of your professors older guys, standing up teaching you and telling you what to do? What is the difference? It's virtually the identical format as church. Do you listen to them and respect them?"

"Well yea," he answered "but that's different."

I pointed out to him the only reason he did not like the format of church was because of his own bias, his attitude against God. At this point, unlike many of the young people I speak with, he lowered his head and admitted I was right. I knew we needed to get back to the first subject he had brought up, so we began talking about why he did not want to have anything to do with Jesus and about the lifestyle he was now living.

We discussed that for quite some time, going back and forth about why he just couldn't live the way he wanted to live. Then he said, "Why can't I just live how I want to live now? How is that any of God's business? I want to have my fun now then maybe someday I will come to God."

I told him first that he was not promised tomorrow, much less four or five years later to come to God. And secondly, that the only way he would be able to do that would be to harden his heart, because God would continue to deal with him and pursue him. I told him he could not imagine the immense danger involved in hardening his heart to that degree.

"Tim, the Bible says that today is the day of salvation, now is the acceptable time and, *Today, if you hear His voice: do not harden your hearts, as in the rebellion.*" [1]

I very gently told him that no matter how he might justify it, the Bible had just identified what was in his heart—rebellion. His reaction to this was amazing. His defiance seemed to go out like air let out of a balloon. He ducked his head and began to nod in agreement. "I never thought of it that way. I know that's true."

"Oh Tim, don't live that way. You are gambling with your eternal soul. The Bible talks about people who abandon the faith and sear their conscience over as with a hot iron. The Bible talks about people who live for pleasure and are dead while they live. In other words, they murder their own conscience."

Then I shared another scripture from Hebrews that outlined his exact attitude toward Jesus, and the tragic results that would follow. *If we deliberately keep on sinning after we have received the knowledge of the truth, no sacrifice for sins is left, but only a fearful expectation of judgment and of raging fire that will consume the enemies of God. Anyone who rejected the law of Moses died without mercy on the testimony of two or three witnesses. How much more severely do you think a man deserves to be punished who has trampled the Son of God under foot, who has treated as an unholy thing the blood of the covenant that sanctified him, and who has insulted the Spirit of grace? (Hebrews 10:26-29).*

I referred to my wife, who was sitting nearby, and said, "Tim, what if I would have said to her early in our relationship, 'Well, you are my girl friend, but right now I don't want to have anything to do with you. I'm going to act as if I don't even know you. I'm going to go out and get drunk and have sex with all the other women I can. I'm just going to have fun. Maybe in four or five years I'll come back and marry you. Will that be OK?'

"First of all, think about the hurt I would be inflicting on her. Secondly, consider how I would have to harden my heart so hard to be able to actually do that. Do you really think that would not damage, if not completely destroy, that relationship? That's what you need to realize. You're not leaving a religion, you're leaving a relationship."

Again he seemed deeply moved, "I know you're right. I know you're right." So then I spoke with him at length about the glorious sacrifice Jesus made at the cross. I pleaded with him not to take the blood of the Savior for granted, to stop and consider the inconceivable love of someone who died a tortuous death in his place. I asked him to think hard about what it must be like for Jesus to have that priceless sacrifice thrown so carelessly back in His face. I encouraged him to get things right with God and shared with him how he could do that.

We talked about 45 minutes. He seemed like a different young man than when we first started talking. He thanked me for telling him the truth. There's not a doubt in my mind that we got through to Tim. We had prayed before we walked on campus for God to show us the one lost sheep. I believe He did!

I have been talking to young people outside the walls of the church for more than twenty-five years. The young people I talk to today are so much more hardened against God than the ones I spoke to twenty years ago. In my ministry on college campuses, I encounter these young people in their natural element. Without the sheltering influence of mom, dad, or their youth pastor nearby, they tell me exactly what is in their heart. I hear precisely what they really think—what their belief system is really all about. Jesus said, ***Out of the abundance of the heart, the mouth speaks.***[2]

28

I spoke with this particular young man in North Carolina, but he is representative of thousands more just like him all over this nation. He is a typical kid, raised in church, now off at college! He is just one of millions in this generation who are swallowing the arsenic-laced lies of the enemy of their souls. Apparently, two-thirds of young people now in church have no intention of staying there. What is even more alarming is we are actually losing **far more** than that.

For quite some time, multiple surveys have indicated about 85% of young people raised in church depart the faith during university years. Now, sadly we're losing even more ground. Many experts have estimated that figure is now approaching **ninety-four percent!!! (94%)**.[3] That should alarm us! Other Christian leaders believe that if current trends continue, within 5-7 years the Christian population of America will only consist of four percent (4%).[4] We are not very far at all behind Europe's godless society.

The Blame Game

As I began researching this book, I encountered a reaction I had not expected. When speaking to friends and church groups about the very delicate and personal subject of people's children and the grave spiritual danger many of them are in, some parents became defensive. Others wanted to pin the blame on the failures of the modern church. However, I believe we must recognize this *defensive posture* can do nothing but paralyze us and keep us from the more important work of prayerfully finding a solution. Whether we are parents or pastors we must humble **ourselves** and be willing to ask some tough questions. At this stage, figuring out who is to blame is immaterial; there is likely plenty of blame to go around. However, what we must do is see the bigger picture. Ultimately it is not the kids, culture, parents, church, nor the educational system, but a far more capable enemy who is responsible.

The Bible declares, *For we do not wrestle against flesh and blood, but against principalities, against powers, against the rulers of the darkness of this age, against spiritual hosts of wickedness in the heavenly places (Ephesians 6:12 NKJV).* No human beings, no matter how dedicated to evil, could possibly orchestrate the culmination of factors that are wreaking so much spiritual havoc and destruction in this generation of precious young souls. Despite the fact that this spiritual warfare is truly raging all around us and inflicting very real casualties on this generation of young people, we must take courage and run to the battle before it is too late! We must engage the real enemy on all possible fronts. But even in the face of such a monumental conflict we do not have to lose heart. Paul indicated that the weapons of our warfare are mighty through God, to the pulling down of strongholds.[5]

We will expose the enemy's hidden and entrenched positions within our culture. Then we will once again look at the overwhelmingly redemptive nature of our God, and the awesome weapons He has provided for us to rescue and restore the young people we love.

This is not so much a book about church growth trends or a sterile retelling of the clinical statistics; it is about a generation of young people losing their souls! It is meant to be a wakeup call for every genuine Christian who loves both the Lord Jesus and the precious young people who are being swept away. It is a call to care and care deeply. To make a difference before it is too late!

O my people, hear my teaching; listen to the words of my mouth. I will open my mouth in parables, I will utter hidden things, things from of old—what we have heard and known, what our fathers have told us. We will not hide them from their children; we will tell the next generation the praiseworthy deeds of the Lord, his power, and the wonders he has done. Psalm 78:1-4

Chapter 4

Lower Education

I remember taking my five year old nephew to his first day of school. He seemed so little and innocent, the very picture of vulnerability. Even though my wife and I were not his parents, we tried to fill in the spiritual gap in his life. We had put a lot into him during his first few years. When he was just a baby, I used to carry him around in my backyard, praying over him. We had taken him to church since he was in diapers, and we even arranged to have him dedicated to the Lord at a worship service. We had talked with him about Jesus and read him Bible stories. We had done all we knew to do to insure his spiritual well-being.

But now as I walked him to that first public school classroom and gave him to his teacher, my emotions began to unravel. I walked back through the noisy hall, out the door, and to my car. As I drove away I could not hold it together any longer; I could not help but weep. I was so aware that kids themselves can mercilessly heap cruelty and teasing on other kids. I also knew there could be bullies, and I hoped his experiences with those elements of growing up would be minimal.

What really troubled me most was that I knew instinctively we had just handed over a great deal of control and influence to the public education system. His first teacher seemed nice enough, but did the overall system have his best interest at heart? Would their version of *his best interest* be anything akin to my deepest held beliefs as an evangelical Christian?

I wished I could be sure there would be no spiritual pitfalls and that I could trust the public school system, but I had a real sense of foreboding. As a Christian, I knew how precious that little heart and mind truly was and how much was at stake. Perhaps I could be accused of taking all this a little too seriously. I can almost hear someone saying, *Lighten up man, you were just taking the kid to school.*

So Much at Stake

When you have seen and heard what I have, it is difficult to see it any other way. Even an op-ed piece in the *New York Times* revealed an understanding of the gravity of a typical day in a public school teacher's life. "...Shaping minds, a moral force in the lives of the young people they teach and know, and in some ways the architects of the future of the nation."[1] Add to this knowledge our Biblical convictions and you see how important the equation really is. The Bible teaches that *bad company corrupts good morals.*[2] The Bible clearly teaches that those morals have an effect not only on our earthly life, but on our eternal existence. We know that there will be a Day of Judgment when every living soul will stand before God and give an account of his life. They will spend eternity in either paradise or torment!

Taking all this into account, you realize how important that educator's **mind shaping moral force** really is. It is a sacred trust! We are exposing our children's minds to educators for six hours a day, twelve to sixteen years of their life! In fact, we must realize that once we put them into the public school system, they will effectively be adults when they are finished. In other words, they are not completely yours to mold ever again. Where their values and beliefs are concerned, you will only be one voice among many competing forces.

As a Christian, we cannot ignore the spiritual minefield our children's educational process has become. So much is at stake. We must see the very real dangers lurking there both physically and spiritually. We must do all to protect their tender spirits as they pass through that labyrinth before entering adulthood.

The fact that many of our children have to pass through a metal detector as they enter the *school house* these days paints a very real picture for us about the dangers they face as they learn to read and write. In just the last few decades, essentially since the nineteen-sixties, when our government very deliberately kicked God out of the educational system, our schools have gone from being a playground to being a battleground (school shootings)! Surely by now no one could be naïve enough to think of the public school system as a neutral landscape devoid of spiritual consequences while our children receive their education. We just cannot afford to have that level of trust in our day.

When condoms are already part of the curriculum, and any reference to God (no matter how innocent) by a teacher within a public school classroom quite literally becomes a federal case, the handwriting is on the wall. Even something as innocuous as **Merry Christmas** sends the left's *secular progressive* storm troopers into action. From Pennsylvania, to Texas, to California, children are now forced to celebrate Islam, sing songs from other world religions and chant the virtues of Kwanzaa. Yet prayer, the Bible, and the content of Christmas carols are treated like hate crimes![3]

California lawmakers have already passed a bill mandating *gay friendly* text books in their public schools. Children as young as kindergarten will be required to learn about the positive contributions to American society by gays, lesbians, and transgender people. As California is one of the nation's leading buyers of textbooks, they set standards with publishers for many other states.

Sadly, in the late eighties, one of our government's highest officials began advocating teaching rather graphic sexual education to children throughout the educational system, even to students as young as kindergarten. He even intended to include non-heterosexual methods and AIDS education. He envisioned making an animated cartoon featuring two condoms, with little faces, who would talk about sex education. Pundits and liberals heaped praise on him as a heroic man of integrity standing up for the truth. The rationale used to foist this perversion on our tiny children was AIDS awareness.[4]

Conservative parents who did not embrace this nonsense and even dared to object to someone teaching their children about sodomy were branded as un-scientific prudes. They were said to be *uncomfortable with the science of reproduction.*[5]

The agenda by some in the educational system to rape our children's souls of all innocence is not hidden very well anymore. They cannot stand our Jesus, they do not like our conservative morals, and they will do all they can to separate our children from those values at the earliest possible age. We must be vigilant.

A Taste of Humanism

The ferocious predator hidden right in the public educational system, lying in wait, crouched and ready to devour our children's soul is not hard to identify. It is none other than the serpent from the Garden of Eden – no surprise there. He has now slithered right into the very fabric of the educational system, tempting our kids with his same **UN**-original lie, **"Did God really say?"** [6] His seductive voice still calls to this latest generation, *Don't trust the God of the Bible to be your moral guide. You as the human are more qualified to make your own decisions about right and wrong.*

The humanists published their blatant agenda to greedily swallow up your child's soul in the clearest possible terms in 1983:

> *I am convinced that the battle for humankind's future must be waged and won in the public school classroom by teachers who correctly perceive their role as the proselytizers of a new faith: a religion of humanity that recognizes and respects the spark of what theologians call divinity in every human being. These teachers must embody the same selfless dedication as the most rabid fundamentalist preachers, they will be ministers of another sort, utilizing a classroom instead of a pulpit to convey humanists values in whatever subject they teach, regardless of the educational level—preschool day care or large state university. The classroom must and will become an arena of conflict between the old and the new— the rotting corpse of Christianity, together with all its adjacent evils and misery, and the new faith of humanism. It will undoubtedly be a long, arduous, painful struggle replete with much sorrow and many tears, but humanism will emerge triumphant (Emphasis added).*[7]

Mixed Up Students

The great banner of humanism is RELATIVE TRUTH. They wave it in our children's faces from pre-school to graduate school. This philosophy dethrones God, exalts humans as the ultimate authority, and screams that nothing is really right or wrong! Everyone can decide for themselves what is right and wrong. With the exception of many fine brave Christian educators, this philosophy has permeated our educational system.

We must realize that the greatest danger lies within. Especially by the time our kids reach their teens, this philosophy is incredibly enticing. So you as parents must truly **FORM** them in their formative years. It is their greatest hope!

In the sixties, *the ungodly left* began to corrupt our educational system. Now for almost four decades we have cranked out students with no moral compass. Today we are eating the fruit of our *secular* society. Not everyone likes the taste. Look how far we have come! An exasperated Houston area school teacher blurts out in a news interview, "By the time I get them in the 9th grade they have already been sexually active in middle school, and some even in early elementary, and people don't want to hear that." [8]

When we fail to provide moral boundaries for our students, the results are disastrous. In the Dallas area not long ago, a nineteen year old girl ran over and killed her waitress in the parking lot of a restaurant to avoid paying the $100 tab she and her friends had just ran up. School shootings like Columbine show us the tragic by-product, when young people are taught that nothing is right or wrong and each person can set their own moral boundaries.

Before I proceed any further, let me acknowledge that there are countless thousands of Christian teachers scattered throughout the education system. The Christian public school teachers that I know personally do everything they can to be a positive influence on the students they teach. However, they are largely muzzled by straight jacket interpretations of the Establishment Clause of the Constitution, despite the fact that there is NO actual reference in that document to *separation of church and state.*

There may well be many, many other teachers who, although not Christian themselves, have no humanist agenda to impose upon your child. However, vast numbers of teachers and administrators absolutely **do** buy into the liberal humanist ideology and do all they can to infect their pupils with this deadly anti-Christian philosophy. And it is easily demonstrated that the hierarchy of the educational system is riddled with these ravenous *secular progressive humanists* eager to carry out their long since published battle plan.

When will our society see the destruction we are heaping on our young people's lives by warping their young minds with secular humanism? The Apostle John said many anti-Christ spirits are already in the world.[9] Humanism is really just that. It is an excuse to throw off the entire idea of God's moral law and utterly despise the notion that Jesus Christ is the only way to salvation.

If primary education represents a subtle guerrilla warfare, carried on from the shadows against our children, higher education has become a full frontal assault. This war is waged by a highly trained professional army with huge weapons on a battlefield so violent and deadly that only a few Christian young people actually survive.

Chapter 5

Higher Education—the Graveyard of Belief

Porn and Pedophilia 101

If I asked most parents if they would like to send their child to one of America's most prestigious Ivy League universities, the greater majority would jump at the chance. No doubt their mind would instantly think of the incredible doors of opportunity such an education would bring to their son or daughter, not to mention the stellar career opportunities later. However, very few, if any, would even begin to realize the *real opportunities* awaiting their young adults while at those celebrated institutions.

At one respected major university they would be treated to complimentary gay, straight, and lesbian pornography and students of all ages would get to watch the infamous 1970's porn flick *Deep Throat*. Of course, these are serious studies, all paid for by the university! Students could be treated to a *lecture* by a famed gay porn director, who among many other crude remarks lamented the fact that "the young boy group is not exposed to sex enough." [1]

In the very first chapter of a textbook that has been used at many top universities across America, including state universities, these prestigious institutions give their stamp of approval to *cross-generational sexual encounters* (more commonly known as pedophilia). Just imagine your innocent teenager's young mind absorbing the following:

> *Like communists and homosexuals in the 1950s, boy lovers are so stigmatized that it is difficult to find defenders for their civil liberties, let alone erotic orientation. Consequently the police have feasted on them. Local police, the FBI and watchdog postal inspectors have joined to build a huge apparatus whose sole aim is to wipe out the community of men who love under-aged youth. In twenty years or so when some of the smoke has cleared, it will be much easier to show that these men have been victims of a savage and undeserved witch hunt. A lot of people will be embarrassed by their collaboration with this persecution, but it will be too late to do much good for those men who have spent their lives in prison.[2]*

As shocking as this may be, it is merely the tip of the iceberg of what is being promoted in the name of *higher education* at universities from coast to coast. With the exception of a few truly conservative Christian universities, the entire system appears to have now been hijacked by radical liberals whose only intent seems to be to strip every shred of moral decency from the students under their tutelage. Furthermore, many will not rest until, if it were possible, they murder the soul of every Christian young person who attends their class. They accomplish this by systematically undermining and decimating their faith in God.

Ironically, while most liberals would consider themselves champions in the area of the humanities, many of their beliefs are anything but. A top professor taught that, "To feed a starving child is to exacerbate the world population problem." [3] Another prominent professor went even further. He believes we should all have 28 days to decide if we truly want our newborn infant. He writes, "Newborn-infants, especially if unwanted, are not yet full members of the moral community." [4] So killing any baby within that time frame, he rationalizes, is acceptable. In addition, he believes killing a disabled infant is not simply acceptable and should be allowed, it is "right!" He also believes that sex with animals, although perhaps not normal, should not be considered offensive.[5] Keep in mind that one of the main reasons the university hired this controversial professor was because he was *mainstream*.[6]

The Roman Road in the Wrong Direction

These people are the most celebrated scholars, noted professors, and intellectuals of our day! Perhaps it is difficult for you to imagine how *any* human being could embrace such bizarre and sickening ideas, let alone the people who are responsible for molding the young minds of students. However, the first chapter of Romans spells out in crystal clear terms what happens when people reject their Creator and throw off His moral constraint. They plunge into a spiral of unthinkable degradation and moral decay. And that is what is now on display at the most exalted educational institutions on the planet!

This tragic spiritual downward process described in the book of Romans culminates in one of the most ironic and yet accurate descriptions of human behavior ever written: *For although they knew God, they neither glorified him as God nor gave thanks to him, but their thinking became futile and their foolish hearts were darkened. Although they claimed to be wise, they became fools (Romans 1:21-22).*

Then this 2,000 year old book accurately predicts their slide will next take them into the deviant underworld of homosexual behavior. This prophetic phenomenon is also prominently on display at these once noble places of learning. True academic pursuits have been replaced with *studies* of unchecked sexual perversion. One is no longer limited to courses on economics and engineering, now a smorgasbord of perverse curriculum awaits those hungry for *scholarly knowledge.* Even state universities now offer gay and lesbian studies, like "How to Be Gay: Homosexuality and Initiation." In the course "Queer Acts," dressing in "drag will be encouraged." All of these *studious intellectual* pursuits are geared to contribute to and advance the interests of lesbians, bisexuals, and gay men. Another well-known university even offers a course called "Pornographies ON/Scene." [7] It all seems different than when I went to school. I guess it's no longer the three R's of *reading, 'riting,* and *'rithmatic.*

Just in case students do not get enough of *cross dressing* in class, there are always plenty of extra curricular activities, like g*ay coming out day* and a c*oming out Ball,* complete with door prizes, free refreshments and a *drag fashion show.* If a student is a little low on cash but still has not satisfied his thirst for *academic knowledge,* they need not worry. Recently, I walked into a campus bookstore and noticed a large sign advertising a big sale — 25% off all books in the *Gay and Lesbian section.* A modern university cannot let a little money stand in the way of students filling their impressionable young minds with immoral sewage.

If the fact that college textbooks actually excuse and legitimize pedophilia is a little too abstract, realize the madness does not stop there. One large state university actually had two convicted child sex offenders on staff at the same time. One, a professor, was still drawing his tax funded $138,000 a year salary while he served his prison sentence for repeatedly sexually assaulting three girls ages five, six, and nine.

Wisconsin State Representative Scott Suder appeared on the August 25, 2005 television show, *The O'Reilly Factor* to express his outrage. "Aside from the minimum sentence, the university refuses to fire him. They claim that they have to go through their own internal investigation process <u>to determine whether or not child rape constitutes grounds for dismissal at the university</u>" (Emphasis added). The other convicted child sex offender continued to work on campus while the university reviewed its policy.[8]

I want to state positively that I am not anti-education, nor am I saying that there are not good decent people holding positions at many of these schools. However, the fact that pedophilia and pornography can be allowed and even promoted under the guise of *education* is madness. The fact that these kinds of things are going on within the classrooms inside the ivy-covered walls at our nation's institutions of *higher education* is not the most grievous aspect of it all.

What is far more appalling is that these vile and debase things are the most celebrated standard of *morality* that exists in the thinking of the people running most of these universities. In their minds the highest ideals are *tolerance, open-mindedness*, and *moral relativism*. In practical terms, this all translates into *anything goes*! Homosexuality, pornography, and even pedophilia apparently represent mankind's most crowning virtues to the ones who set the tone of acceptable behavior on many university campuses these days!

Pressure to conform to these *ideals* is so palpable on these campuses that very few muster the courage to publicly challenge them. Those that do are greeted with such a vicious level of sanctimonious contempt as to chase all but the hardiest back into the cave of conformity. The feeding frenzy of snobbish ridicule tends to bludgeon most back into compliant submission. One must either agree with this perverse sense of right and wrong or be ostracized as an old fashioned prude. This same group that can look upon gay porn as a virtue can simultaneously turn abstinence, purity, or motherhood into dirty words.

The Prophet Isaiah of old has a warning for the modern university: *Woe to those who call evil good and good evil, who put darkness for light and light for darkness, who put bitter for sweet and sweet for bitter. Woe to those who are wise in their own eyes and clever in their own sight (Isaiah 5:20-21).* If these things are the tip of the iceberg—things sanctioned by the administrators and *taught* by the faculty— we need only imagine what is going on just under the surface and behind the scenes.

Student Life!

Recently, I read several extremely disturbing magazine articles on the life of college students in America. One article indicated that if parents had any idea what was going on in the name of higher education, *they would get in their cars, drive to campus, and drag their offspring kicking and screaming from their co-ed dorms, frat houses, and rule-free residence halls.*[9] The other article referenced a novelist who is known to research his books with months of careful observation of his subjects. He examined the culture of major universities across America. He paints a picture of a destructive, unhealthy, morally toxic environment, doing unimaginable long-term damage to our children. A world not so much of serious academic study, but rather one of *binge drinking, transgender celebrations*, and *naked parties.*

He tells the story of a bright young girl, raised in church by caring parents, who innocently goes off to university. Slowly, she is dragged into the cesspool of degradation and promiscuity—a culture in which dating and traditional courtship are replaced by *hooking up*, totally impersonal sex, separated from both commitment and relationship.[10]

What creates such an unhealthy environment? It is ultimately the college administrators themselves. Even in 1957, Clark Kerr, chancellor of the University of California at Berkeley, quipped that *his job responsibilities were "providing parking for faculty, sex for students, and athletics for the alumni."* [11] Those attitudes have run unchecked for decades now, bringing us to the almost unequaled depravity we find today.

This article, written by a professor from Loyola University, decried what he called, "The sex carnival that is college life today." He compared American college co-ed dorms to brothels. He went on to say:

> "There is nothing new or novel about human depravity or debauchery. Outrage over debauchery is deserved. Nevertheless, as I have suggested already, my outcry is not directed at the debauchery among college students, but rather at the colleges themselves. Today colleges not only turn a blind eye to this behavior, but also set up the conditions that foster and invite it. I am concerned about the young men and women who wish to behave differently, but for whom this is made especially difficult by the living conditions their colleges provide and often insist upon....
>
> "This is the grisly underbelly of the modern American college; the deep, dark, hidden secret that many parents suspect is there but would rather not face. The long-term damage to our children is difficult to measure. But it is too obvious to deny. I remember once hearing that the British lost the empire when they started sending their children away to boarding schools. I do not know whether anyone has ever seriously proposed that thesis. I am prepared, however, to ask whether America might not be lost because the

great middle class was persuaded that they must send their children to college with no questions asked, when in fact this was the near-equivalent of committing their sons and daughters to one of the circles of Dante's Inferno." [12]

Chapter 6

Re-education Camps

In the former Soviet Union, if a family were discovered to be Christian, mom and dad would likely be shipped off to a gulag in Siberia. Their children would be taken away and sent to a re-education camp, where they would be brainwashed back into good Marxists. Although the Soviet Union may have collapsed, it seems their re-education camps have been largely relocated to America. The only major difference is we voluntarily send our kids to receive a Marxist education and pay for the privilege through tax dollars and tuition.

This may seem a bold assertion, but when you look at what is going on, it is the only plausible conclusion. Read the writings of the most celebrated professors, look at the books on the required reading list and it is not difficult to figure out the prevailing philosophy being force-fed to the American college population. It doesn't exactly take a sleuth to see they are being served a steady diet of unvarnished Marxism. In case you think I've lost my train of thought and this part of the book seems to be more political than spiritual in nature, remember that one of the major tenets of Marxism is atheism. As I have already stated, all of this is part of one mammoth iceberg.

While reading Howard Zinn's *A People's History of the United States*, which is assigned at universities across the nation, students can learn that America's founding fathers diabolically created a system of government to ensure riches for themselves, while simultaneously crafting a scheme to repress and control all the citizens of the future country. Amazingly, Zinn credits Maoist China with the closest system on earth to a free people's government. He also *teaches* our kids that America was to blame for World War II, not Hitler's Nazis or Japan's bombing of Pearl Harbor.

All those things it seems were cleverly concocted illusions; the real cause was Uncle Sam's hunger for empire. World War II was his grand scheme to colonize! America's most notable achievements, like first in flight and the walk on the moon; her greatest inventors; her most important battles, like Gettysburg and D-day; along with Lincoln's Gettysburg Address, are all conspicuously left out entirely. However, if you want pages and pages on the My Lai massacre in Vietnam and other alleged American missteps and atrocities, this is your book.[1]

Whether you are reading *A People's History of the United States* or the meanderings of MIT's Noam Chomsky, or the host of other books students **must** read, the message is always the same. The former Soviet Union, China, and Cuba are bastions of freedom with a higher standard of living than our own, while America is a seething pot of repression and bloody human rights violations, set on colonizing the world.

No matter where the facts actually point, America is always the villain destroying the environment of Mother Earth and oppressing the rest of mankind. The rest of the world is good, benevolent, and always right on every issue. From Islamic fascism to China's human rights record, the historical facts are always presented exactly backward to actual reality—to make America, capitalism, and most of all Christianity look bad.

In radical Islam, America is seen as the *Great Satan*! It is also obviously a major tenet of the faith on most liberal campuses. Imagine being the son or daughter of a U.S. military officer and seeing the email a New Jersey college professor sent to one of his students containing the following statement: *Real freedom will come when soldiers in Iraq turn their guns on their superiors and fight for just causes and for people's needs.*[2]

There could not be a better example of a left wing America-basher than the bizarre and infamous Ward Churchill. This *University of Colorado* professor wrote an essay on September 11, 2001, that later became part of a book. "The most that can honestly be said of those involved on Sept 11, is that they finally responded in kind to some of what this country has dispensed to their people as a matter of course." Then to add **immense insult** to injury, imagine the victims who lost loved ones in the World Trade Center towers hearing Mr. Churchill's next chilling words. "Well, really let's get a grip here shall we? True enough, they were civilians of a sort. But innocent? Gimme a break... If there was a better, more effective, or in fact any other way of visiting some penalty befitting their participation upon the little Eichmanns inhabiting the sterile sanctuary of the twin towers, I'd really be interested in hearing about it."[3]

Thousands of men and women died tragic fiery premature deaths on 9/11. Some unable to bear the intensity of the heat and flames leapt to the concrete a hundred stories below. On that very day this *scholar* compared all those victims to the architect of the Nazi Holocaust, and in effect said they got what they deserved. Why? His callous rational was purely based on the fact that they were – Americans.

These are the *educators* to whom we entrust our children's minds. Every day they abuse their power and tenured positions to warp the thinking of impressionable young pupils. And more often than not, their salary is paid for by our tax dollars.

Coercion & Intimidation

From the moment many modern students arrive at college, they must attend tolerance and sensitivity training where they have to learn their university's *speech codes*. This is the first shot across the bow, laying down the gauntlet that straying from the politically correct path will ironically not be **tolerated**. It doesn't take long to figure out that tolerance only includes liberal politically correct viewpoints. Like any good re-education camp, coercion and intimidation are the necessary tools to insure compliance. If you have ever been verbally bullied and belittled by a liberal intellectual, then you would understand what a conservative or a Christian college student faces most every day.

As a vocal Christian, I have experienced this more times than I can count. The elitist *Mode of Operation* usually involves a few snide remarks about anyone else's low intelligence compared to their gifted and enlightened mind, often followed by a condescending layer of mock pity for everyone else's ignorance. As a secure Christian adult I wear their contempt as a badge of honor for my Lord Jesus Christ! Armed with the sturdy wisdom and truth of God's eternal Word, I feel no sense of shame whatsoever about my faith in the God of the Bible. But that is all easy enough for me; I'm not nineteen years old and my tormentor is not grading my paper.

For the average eighteen or nineteen year old freshman, standing up against this intimidation is all but impossible. Add to this the fact that the greater majority of the student body has not been raised with any kind of Christian values and so happily go along with the program. This, combined with the *authority figure intimidation*, creates a storm surge of peer pressure that simply drowns all but the sturdiest Christian kids. The pressure to conform is simply enormous; it must feel like trying to swim up Niagara Falls.

About half of all students surveyed on this subject said their professors injected political and social views into the curriculum, even in classes that had nothing to do with those subjects. And one third of students in the same survey said they feel they have to agree with their professors political and social views in order to get a good grade. News interviews with students confirm this intimidating pressure to comply.[4]

"If the professor has a Leftist opinion in class, students feel very fearful of making a comment to counter that" — UC Berkeley student.[5]

"Most students are here to get an education, and would rather participate in the brainwashing and pass the class than fight back." — Foothills College student.[6]

"(Students are) ...afraid of expressing their own minds, because the guy who is going to be grading your paper, giving you your final grade, believes that your opinions are insane..." — UC Berkeley student.[7]

The experience of another young freshman attending Foothills College near San Francisco highlights the extreme measures some professors will go to badger dissenting students into compliance. The Kuwaiti born student was eager to learn the governmental system of the *land of the free*, so he registered for *Introduction to American Government and Politics*. He was shocked by his professor's daily one-sided America-bashing lectures.

Ultimately, his final take home exam consisted of one essay: *Dye and Zeigler contend that the Constitution of the United States was not "ordained and established" by "the people" as we have so often been led to believe. They contend instead that it was written by a small educated and wealthy elite in America who were representative of powerful economic and political interests. Analyze the US Constitution (Original document), and show how its formulation excluded the majority of the people living in America at the time, and how it was dominated by America's elite interest.*[8]

Talk about leading the witness! The verbiage was so narrow that the only way to answer this question correctly would have been to join in the anti-American rant. So Ahmad did just the opposite. He summoned his courage and did the unthinkable. Instead, he wrote an essay defending America's founding fathers and praising the US Constitution as a document promoting extraordinary freedom.

Naturally, this kind of thinking could not be **tolerated** by the high-minded professor. So instead of grading the paper, Ahmad was instead ordered to his office. There he was berated and told his views about the greatness of our country were irrational and naïve. "America is not God's gift to the world," he was told. Then the professor really tightened down the screws.

The college freshman was then told he needed *regular psychotherapy*. His professor then threatened to report him to the Dean of International Admissions if he did not submit to the treatment.[9] The young man knew this dean had power to revoke his student visa. I'm sure even the Soviet re-education camps would have been impressed by this level of coercion! A diagnosis of mental instability could certainly have long reaching negative ramifications on a young man's life, much less the threat of deportation.

It worked. The young man left the office terrified over the possibility of being deported for writing his pro-American essay. He immediately made the appointment with the school psychologist. Thankfully, that is where his nightmare stopped. After her evaluation of him she determined he in no way needed psychotherapy. His story eventually found its way into the media, even making it into the pages of some national newspapers. Other students of the same professor emailed and called one of the columnists to confirm the brainwashing tactics applied by this *hateful* professor.

Chapter 7

A Legion of Atheistic Professors Await!

Liberally Lopsided

No good indoctrination camp worth its salt would be fair and balanced in its presentation of *the facts*. True to form, America's university system makes sure everything stays liberally lopsided. Although the great catch-word thrown about in excess at major universities is **diversity**, that is in actual fact a joke! This liberal lopsidedness even caught the attention of the *Washington Post*. A March 29, 2005 story began: *College faculties, long assumed to be a liberal bastion, lean further to the left than even the most conspiratorial conservatives might have imagined, a new study says.*[1]

On most campuses, the ratio of liberal to conservative administrators and faculty is about ten to one. However, at the nation's top schools, that figure runs as high as thirty to one.[2] The phenomenon of liberal indoctrination lives on within academia. The vastly outnumbered Christian professors are virtually muzzled and their influence marginalized. One such professor commented in a magazine article:

> **"As a Christian and professional educator, I walk a tightrope. While colleagues may freely explore Buddhist beliefs or left-wing politics, Christians are limited in the ways we can practice and model our faith at state universities. Due to restrictive interpretations of the U.S. Constitution's separation of church and state, instructors may not express personal religious views for fear of 'unduly influencing' college students... I must lead them away from scriptural references or personal beliefs to avoid charges of 'proselytizing.' Stories that criticize Christianity, however, are prolific and encouraged."** [3]

Students are often told they are being trained to *question everything*. But the truth is they are trained only to question any conservative values they may hold. Although liberals love to claim they celebrate tolerance and inclusion, believe me, you dare not question their views! Question the morality of homosexuality or abortion, question Darwin's theory of evolution, and they turn into vicious angry attack dogs. Sharks in a feeding frenzy are far more reasonable!

A Trip to Sea World!

Although every university may not be as extreme as the examples I have given, some are definitely better than others. Every university where I have spent time, this same hyper-liberal spirit pervades the entire campus. All this propaganda and pressure has the desired effect—**mindless conformity!** This anti-American, anti-Christian message becomes deeply rooted in the hearts and minds of our youth.

As I speak with the students in the free speech zones of America's universities from Texas to Wisconsin, the Midwest to the east coast, the radical leftist talking points spew from the mouth of most students like broken records. Word for word they parrot their liberal professors. Sadly, going to most college campuses is like taking a trip to Sea World. When the subjects of abortion, homosexuality, radical feminism, anti-American rhetoric, or the evils of the archaic intolerant religion of Christianity are brought up, the trained seal act begins. Heads nod in the affirmative, flippers clap, accompanied by the **obligatory** politically correct response, "Aorrrrrt, aorrrrt aorrrrrt." "Very good Skipper!!!" And a fish is thrown into the student's mouth by the liberal professor!

The High Cost of a College Education

I think we can safely say in American culture today, most couples work a large portion of their adult life just to pay for their children's education. The monetary cost however is truly minimal compared to the real price being extracted. The real cost is the spiritual well-being of millions of kids who grew up in *youth group*, who have now crashed violently against the jagged rocks of a hostile academia.

I have already cited the Loyola professor who said sending kids off to college these days is "the near-equivalent of committing our sons and daughters to one of the circles of Dante's Inferno." I could not agree more. Perhaps without realizing it, Christian parents have sent their kids off to college with no idea of the spiritual graveyard modern universities have become. They have naively thought of college as a spiritually neutral place where their children would simply get an education.

I think now of the countless times I have been approached by someone after I have spoken on the subject of our ministry on college campuses. A mom, dad, or perhaps grandmother has had an almost identical reaction. With a bewildered, even whimsical look, a light dawns and they verbalize the statement as they themselves come to grips with it: "When my son (or daughter or grandchild) went off to college is exactly when he got away from God."

Also for the first time they seem to realize that it was not an isolated incident, but rather a spiritual epidemic killing the souls of millions of young people. Believe me when I say, it is no accident! It is the result of a sinister plan.

Keep Out the Light!

In the last forty years, if you were to stroll the manicured grounds of one of the most respected Ivy League colleges, you would notice something curious as you looked upon its chapel. Even though the lovely old building has been in continuous use, the windows have been boarded up this entire time to prevent anyone from seeing the Christian scenes depicted in the stained glass. They have not done so because a lawsuit citing the separation of church and state was brought by some rabid atheist lawyer. They are a private institution. The windows were boarded up purely from the motive of the school's anti-Christian bigotry.

Even though the windows have not been physically boarded up at all universities, it certainly paints a picture of the attitude most of them have adopted. Board up those windows, we must keep the light of God out of here! The most notable universities in the world, including Harvard, Cambridge, Yale, Princeton, and Dartmouth, to name a few, were all founded by Christians to train ministers. In most cases, they not only have turned their backs on their heritage, they have now become seedbeds of hostility directed against the God of the Bible.

Nationwide, Christian groups on campus must fight running battles against discrimination. Many of these groups have been banned or lost their status because they are accused of being discriminatory in nature. In other words, if a homosexual atheist wants to be an officer in your Christian club, he must be allowed to do so or your group will be banned. Thankfully, some fine legal watchdog groups have arisen and won back the right of many of these groups to exist.

But it is an uphill battle for the believer in Jesus. In Florida, a Christian student group was forbidden to show the movie, *The Passion of the Christ*, because it was R-rated. (No matter that some schools have whole courses on porn.) This exact same school administration did, however, allow a theater group to stage a play, with an atrociously offensive title that included the name of Jesus along with a vulgar sexual reference. And the play itself depicted actors simulating sexual acts with Jesus himself. Many who had seen the play had the opinion that had this play been a movie, it would have easily earned an X rating. I often tell parents that to send their child to a typical state university is sending them into the razor sharp blades of a liberal meat grinder.

Targets of Extreme Intimidation

A legion of atheistic professors is awaiting our church kids. They gleefully delight in obliterating the faith of young people in their class. A student emailed his campus newspaper with the following observation. **"As a young man still in college I am astounded not only by the number of students that haven't heard the gospel but by the number of professors that strive every day to poison the minds of anyone who might be open to the message of the gospel."**

It is easy to see who bears the brunt of the unkind ridicule and liberal indoctrination on the average college campus. More than anyone else, Christians are the target of predatory persecution! One observer said, "We are consistently seeing that conservative Christians are not exactly the darlings of university administrations. A host of injustices are being visited against these groups," prompting even the U.S. Department of Education to note *intentional discrimination and harassment.*[4] Despite this fact, a steady tide of cruel anti-Christian rhetoric daily crashes against the soul of our young people who have been raised in church. For those trying to hold on to their beliefs, the damage is done. Like a turbulent swift current eroding away a sandy riverbank, the fragile faith of an eighteen year old fresh out of youth group cannot withstand the tide of ungodly influence.

The more students and former students I speak with, the clearer the picture emerges of exactly what is going on in the classrooms. Christian students experience extreme intimidation daily from their elitist professors. These professors seem to relish the near dictatorial control they have over their young charges.

I've heard so many students say that every day, regardless of the subject matter of the course, the liberal professor starts off with a rant. This tirade lasts half the class time and is directed against conservatives or the brainless Christians who hold on to their archaic superstitious faith in God despite all the scientific evidence. A young woman told me recently that the message communicated daily is, *No one with intelligence can believe in God. Faith is pure superstition made up by weak-minded people. It is their crutch because they are too stupid to stand on their own.* She also told me how much her faith was impacted by this daily barrage from these authority figures. A female student who wanted to be a missionary emailed J. Budziszewski, author of **How to Stay Christian in College,** to say that *although her anthropology professor was kind and gentlemanly when discussing non-Christian religions, he suddenly turned harsh and vulgar when the subject turned to Christianity.*[5]

These anti-Christian bigots certainly feel no need to constrain themselves to *the truth*. First of all, they do not believe in the concept of truth, so pure fabrication means nothing to them. Not only do I constantly hear their talking points from their students, I have on occasion tangled with them myself in the free speech zones of the universities where I speak. Their seething hatred of God and all things Christian inspires them to distortions of church history and Biblical themes so outlandish that they would have made the Nazi propagandist, Joseph Goebbels, blush.

Here are some that come up **daily** as I debate on campus:

∞ *The Bible promotes slavery, racism, rape, murder, and all war.*

∞ *Jesus was a misunderstood homosexual who never claimed to be the Son of God.*

∞ *The Bible was written five hundred years after Jesus by greedy, power-hungry church fathers for their own personal and political gain.*

Do any of these *educators* ever offer evidence that could withstand rebuttal from anyone with knowledge in these areas? No, of course they don't; first of all, because 99% of their young students have no clue about most of these subjects, and secondly, they don't need to. These professors are authority figures who hold the future of their students in their hands. Most students consider the opinion of the scholarly sage standing at the front of their classroom to be **gospel.**

The outnumbered, outgunned Christians squirm and endure this daily artillery barrage, hunkered down in the foxhole of silence, keeping their views to themselves. They begin to struggle with doubt, haunted by all the high sounding arguments their professors put forth.

Naturally, there is no room for anyone presenting the other side of the argument. The most grounded and rugged young believers are able to fight past those demons. The vast majority of *church kids* are simply spiritually trampled to death. The Day of Judgment is going to be a messy affair for many of the professors of anti-religious bigotry. Jesus has a warning they would do well to heed: ***But whoever causes one of these little ones who believe in Me to stumble, it is better for him that a heavy millstone be hung around his neck, and that he be drowned in the depth of the sea (Matthew 18:6 NASB).***

I want to say that I have no disrespect for professors in general; as a matter of fact, some of my closest friends and colleagues are college professors. I deeply respect people who have dedicated their lives to education. I can think of few professions that could be more rewarding than that of imparting valuable knowledge to hungry young minds! What is truly reprehensible though is that so much of our tax-funded system of higher education has been high jacked by people who hate God and Christianity with a passion and use their tenured positions to poison the minds of our kids.

The Spirit of the Anti-Christ on Campus

Would your church hire a sexually promiscuous student minister who passed out condoms and literature promoting that lifestyle? Would your church consider calling a pastor who was an avowed atheist and very pointedly railed against the existence of God? Of course not, we would not think of entrusting our kids to such people. However, what is happening is that in the space of a few weeks when our kids leave the church youth group and become college freshmen, they are thrown into a world where most of their authority figures hate the very notion of the existence of God.

At the very least, as Christians, we need to withdraw our admiration and respect from these once venerable institutions of learning. They are not what they used to be. Unfortunately, our system of higher education has to a large degree become cancerous. This is having a devastating affect on America's ill-prepared impressionable young students.

If you are a Christian parent, you are faced with many difficult decisions concerning your child's education. The spiritual well-being of your child should be at the top of the list as you consider their college. We as Christians should support the universities that hold a truly Biblical worldview. At the very least, churches, pastors, youth workers, and parents should purpose to prepare our young people for what they will face before they go off to college.

My wife and I know firsthand that most university campuses are brimming with an anti-christ spirit. We have looked into the tormented faces of those whose faith has been decimated. This keeps our hearts motivated to go and be a voice crying out in this wilderness called *university*. The early disciples of Jesus courageously declared HIS Word to the pagan world of their time. They were accused of turning that world upside down! Pray for young people you may know who are off at college or who soon will be. Pray for a great awakening, a revival, a true counter-revolution on the college campuses of America!

Chapter 8

Teach Your Children

Practical Ways to Protect Your Children's Spiritual Health

I'm sure by this point you must realize how important it is to insulate our children from the destructive pitfalls laid for them in today's culture. We would not dream of sending our little ones out the door on a freezing cold day without a good heavy coat to protect them from the elements. Similarly, we need to protect them spiritually when we send them out into a harsh cold world full of ungodly influences. How can we best do that?

First, I would say, dedicate your children to the Lord. It may seem like such a small thing, but I believe God honors it immensely. There is something very powerful about publicly consecrating children to the Lord. Normally in church we call it *baby dedication*. That certainly is the best possible time to do it, before the world has a chance to exert its influence upon them.

I have seen older children dedicated to the Lord by parents who have become believers and understand how important that simple act of faith is. If you have never dedicated your children to the Lord, if at all possible, take this step with God. Even though my family did not attend church regularly, they took me as an infant to my grandmother's church and had me dedicated to the Lord. I believe that is, at least in part, why I serve God today.

God's perfect plan is for whole families to serve Him! When the distraught jailer in Philippi cried out to Paul and Silas, "Sirs, what must I do to be saved?" God's anointed messengers confidently told him, *"Believe in the Lord Jesus, and you will be saved—you and your household."* Then amazingly, well after midnight, they preached the Gospel to everyone in the jailer's house and baptized all of them. The Bible records, *The jailer brought them into his house and set a meal before them; he was filled with joy because he had come to believe in God—he and his whole family.*[1]

Scripture is perfectly clear; faith is most effectively passed on from one generation to the next by the godly family. The Old and New Testaments reinforce this abiding principle over and over again, as we shall see. Paul recognized this in his most beloved helper, young Timothy: *I have been reminded of your sincere faith, which first lived in your grandmother Lois and in your mother Eunice and, I am persuaded, now lives in you also (2 Timothy 1:5).*

What's a Parent to Do?

We must seize the opportunity to truly form children during their formative years. Wonderfully, it is not some mysterious process beyond the comprehension of all but the super spiritual. God's Word is enormously practical on exactly how we are to do this.

I was recently reading the Bible and a passage seemed to leap from the page at me. Its clarity and utter practicality made it impossible to ignore. It pertained to the diligence

God expects of us in passing on the faith to our children. *Fix these words of mine in your hearts and minds; tie them as symbols on your hands and bind them on your foreheads. Teach them to your children, talking about them when you sit at home and when you walk along the road, when you lie down and when you get up. Write them on the doorframes of your houses and on your gates, so that your days and the days of your children may be many in the land that the Lord swore to give your forefathers, as many as the days that the heavens are above the earth (Deuteronomy 11:18-21).*

We must first of all be diligent in our own devotional life. I like how the New American Standard Bible rendered the first phrase of the text: *You shall therefore impress these words of mine on your heart and on your soul.* We are instructed to impress God's Word on our own heart and mind. We cannot teach our children what we ourselves do not know. It is much like when you listen to the safety instructions on a commercial airliner shortly before takeoff. You are always instructed that should there be a sudden loss of cabin pressure and the oxygen masks drop, to secure your own mask first then afterward help your child. If you lose consciousness you are going to be of no use to your child. Likewise, we must also be diligent to take in God's Word for our own spiritual health, and then we can teach our children.

The reference to binding His Words on our hands and foreheads refers to the Hebrew custom of physically wearing small leather boxes, called phylacteries, with a portion of scripture inside. I believe in modern application that means God's Word must have a public and prominent place in our lives.

It should be obvious to anyone who knows us, that the message of the New Testament is the single greatest influence shaping our life and character. Your work colleagues, friends, and neighbors should see your faith in God's Word, but more than anyone else, your children should see this beautiful process played out in your life.

Many of us have been programmed to believe *faith is a personal thing*. In other words, it is inappropriate to speak about it except in its proper place, like church. But Jesus did not teach that. Instead He said, *If anyone is ashamed of me and my words, the Son of Man will be ashamed of him when he comes in his glory (Luke 9:26a).* Our love and regard for God's Word should be on display at all times, especially at home.

Secondly, we must have a **lifestyle** of unashamedly talking about God and His Word everywhere we go. Again, note God's unmistakable and practical exhortation as to where we should be teaching our children about our faith in Christ: *Teach them to your children, talking about them when you sit at home and when you walk along the road, when you lie down and when you get up. Write them on the doorframes of your houses and on your gates.*

God's Word should not just be in our heart and mind, but on our lips. God shows us plainly that He expects us to teach our children by talking about His Word from morning until night, when we are at home, and when we are away from home. Not only that, He tells us to write it on the doorframes of your houses and gates. Again, we see it is not just internal, but on display publicly. Our life should be brimming full, actually overflowing, with God's Word, and our children should see this.

This is God's tried and true way of forming their character. If we all aimed at obeying this concept, not only would our kids be solidly drawn into the Kingdom of our Lord Jesus, we would turn the world upside down! To some, this lifestyle of being committed to the Word of God may sound like utter fanaticism, but it is God's perfectly revealed will. Some may also tend to dismiss this as Old Testament legalism, but the New Testament calls us to an even more radical commitment: ***Therefore, I urge you, brothers, in view of God's mercy, to offer your bodies as living sacrifices, holy and pleasing to God—this is your spiritual act of worship. Do not conform any longer to the pattern of this world, but be transformed by the renewing of your mind. Then you will be able to test and approve what God's will is—his good, pleasing and perfect will (Romans 12:1-2).***

I love the phrase *do not conform any longer* in verse two. God is so merciful that no matter how we have lived before, we can be transformed and not live a lukewarm life **any longer**. Our Lord Jesus purchased us with His own blood, so He is worthy of our lives. The benefits of living our lives to please the Lord will also overflow into our children's lives. One thing is for sure, if we fail to train our children and mold their beliefs to the Word of the living God, there are plenty of others who will rush in to fill the void. We must be the voice that influences our children toward Jesus—pop culture will not lead them to Him. Their educators are not going to tell them about living a life of faith in God. We must teach our kids about faith.

Since we have seen what ungodly influences have been injected into the secular educational process, we face a real dilemma. Our children have to be educated. I have immense respect for parents who make the enormous commitment and sacrifice of time to home school. Thankfully today, there are more resources than ever to assist those who desire to do this. I interviewed a very dedicated *home school mom* who gave me great insight into all that is available now. Curriculums vary in both scope and price; some are even available at public libraries.

Home school parents can also join co-ops geared to their needs. This a network of parents, usually connected to a local church. Different parents with different skills and talents work together to give the children of the co-op a balanced education as well as social development. If one parent is strong in a certain subject (math, foreign language, etc.) then they utilize this valuable resource.

Co-ops provide much in the area of socialization for the children, as well as offering field trips, P.E., sports, and even fine arts training! Drama, ballet, art, music, choir, and band instruments offer kids great opportunities to learn and have fun. Best of all these co-ops are usually not expensive. Overall, home schooled children average much higher on national tests than children from public schools.[2] The home school mom we talked to said the best part was what she called selective socialization – "You can pick and choose who your children *interact* with, instead of just throwing them to the wolves."

I realize that for a variety of reasons not everyone is able to home school. Private schools are an option but, of course, are more of an economic challenge. Every family must make choices based on their situation and God's leading. Most people, including Christians, will send their children to public school. The most important factor is the matter of **influence!** Who will be molding your child's moral fiber? Your priority must be to make sure **you** are the one shaping their character. This is naturally done best when God's supernatural wisdom, grace, and assistance are working on your behalf. The most practical way for that to happen is for His Word to be the most preeminent thing in your home.

The Bible says we are to be in the world, but not of the world. A monastic life is utterly impossible since we are talking about the subject of families. We are all in the world, including our kids, and in contact with our culture and its influences for hours and hours every day. The only way to counteract the negatives encountered there is by having our heart full of the Word of God. David said, *I have hidden your word in my heart that I might not sin against you (Psalm 119:11).* As your children walk into that first public classroom, prepare them. As they progress through school and they are old enough to grasp the issues involved, guide them and talk to them about what God has to say on every subject they come across.

A Pastor's Advice for Perpetuating the Faith

Remember, the subject at hand is how to best insure that your little ones will follow Christ into adulthood. I recently asked a pastor friend of mine to write a column on this subject for our ministry magazine, *Proclaim.* I include it here in its entirety.

What is God's plan for perpetuating the faith? The answer the church seems to be giving these days is *providing the best children and youth ministries possible in the church.* While it is good to do this, it is not God's plan for perpetuating through the generations. In Exodus, the Lord said to Moses that during the festival days each year, the parents should explain to their children why they were celebrating. *You must explain to your children, "I am celebrating what the Lord did for me when I left Egypt."* [3]

God did not tell Moses to bring all of the children to the Temple or the synagogue to hear the stories about God's wondrous acts, rather, the Lord gives that responsibility to the family. Moms and dads are to tell the children about the wonderful things God has done for the nation and for them individually.

In Deuteronomy 6:6-7, the single-most important scripture to the Hebrew people, the Lord says, *You must commit yourselves wholeheartedly to these commands that I am giving you today. Repeat them again and again to your children. Talk about them when you are at home and when you are on the road, when you are going to bed and when you are getting up (NLT).* It seems that according to the Lord, the family becomes the primary environment for teaching the things of God, His statutes, and His plan for the world.

It is important that the church not look to replace mom and dad when it comes to teaching children about God. Rather, the church needs to come alongside mom and dad, even help them to be able to teach their children about the Lord. God says it is mom and dad's responsibility, so the church should do whatever it takes to help them live out that responsibility and not look to replace them. Having said that, we live in a world in which too many parents have completely relinquished that responsibility. In those cases, the church must take up the slack.

The challenge for the church becomes two-fold. First, the church must teach children all they can about the Lord. It must also teach parents that it is *their* responsibility to teach *their* children about the Lord, not just bring them to church. They must talk with them about God as they live their lives together. Teaching the things of God and perpetuating the faith should happen within the normal activities of our everyday lives.

One of the main problems to be overcome is the compartmentalization of our lives. In our culture, we seem to put everything in their own compartments in our minds. There is the work box, the family box, the fun box, and the God box. God would rather be the one big box that holds our minds, work, family, and fun all together. The Hebrews understood this. Everything in their lives flowed out of their faith. That is our challenge.[4]

Young Hearts are Tender Hearts

It is far more effective to instill godly values in children while they are young. It is far better to plant the seeds of the Gospel in the tender, fertile heart of a four year old than in the heart of a rebellious, sin-entangled twenty year old. We should do all we can to teach children God's Word! *Train a child in the way he should go, and when he is old he will not turn from it (Proverbs 22:6).*

I thank God that is my testimony. Although my family did not go to church much when I was growing up, every night of my life when I was three and four years old, my mother planted the seeds of God's Word in my soft young heart. She would gather me up in her lap at bedtime and read stories from a set of big blue children's Bible books. She read all ten volumes to me. Still lodged in my middle-aged brain today are the rich pictures and beautiful words of my Creator, put there when I was a child.

I remember Adam and Eve, the Garden of Eden, the serpent, the first sin, Noah and his huge ark, and Job's sufferings. But more than anything I remember Jesus and that He loved me so much that He was nailed to a rough wooden cross for my sin. If I close my eyes, I can still see those exact pictures filling my young imagination and heart as my mother read to me the stories of my Savior.

Not until I was seventeen years old did I understand for the first time what it meant to be born again—to be saved. But the moment I heard it, I connected it to the Jesus I had heard about as a little boy. At that point, bowing my knee to Him and giving my whole life to Him was the easiest thing in the world for me, and I've never wanted to turn back.

Fathers, do not exasperate your children; instead, bring them up in the training and instruction of the Lord. Ephesians 6:4

Chapter 9

Sin is Crouching at the Door!

I'll never forget as a young minister being called to the hospital to see a 15 year old boy named Brian, who had been in a serious car accident. My credentials, which I had only recently received, ushered me directly into the surgical intensive care unit at the county hospital. I was ill prepared for what came next. A nurse took me over to his bedside. I looked down at a young man who looked more like a monster than a human being. I had never seen such grotesque swelling, bruising, and seemingly innumerable cuts and abrasions before. He had a gruesome exposed incision from his neck to his navel, freshly stapled shut, left over from the emergency surgery to repair all the internal damage.

Although he was fully conscious, he was unable to speak because he was on a ventilator. But his face told me all I needed to know. On it was a look of stark terror. I introduced myself to him and began trying to think of things to say to bring him some measure of comfort. My own words seemed to bounce off him and mock my efforts. As I leaned over his battered face, I found myself staring into the most terrified eyes I'd ever seen. It was as if his eyes were pleading, even screaming at me for some answer, some reassurance that this would all turn out OK. He was longing for what I knew I could not give him. Something that would reverse the clock and remove him from the horrible nightmare he now found himself in—the tragic results of sin.

I really did not know him at all. I was there because I worked with his aunt and was the only minister the family knew. He and a carload of friends had gone out on a Friday night to party and drink and the driver also became intoxicated. They hit a concrete bridge support going 80 MPH.

I was only permitted a few minutes with him, but I did my best to communicate what it meant for him to put his trust in Jesus Christ. He responded to my words with affirmative hand squeezes at the appropriate points of the conversation. Then I prayed for him. Sadly, his aunt informed me that they amputated his right leg above the knee the next morning.

This young man unfortunately found out firsthand and too late the utter cruelty of sin's consequences. However, our two thousand year old book, that many dismiss as irrelevant, could have saved this young man so much pain, sorrow, and regret. It warns about the dangers of sin and even more specifically, abusing alcohol. *Do not gaze at wine when it is red, when it sparkles in the cup, when it goes down smoothly! In the end it bites like a snake and poisons like a viper (Proverbs 23:31-32).* If only he had heard its warning before his tragedy.

The Brutal Nature of Sin!

Before Cain ever raised a hand to murder his brother Abel, God warned him: *Sin is crouching at your door; it desires to have you, but you must master it (Genesis. 4:7b).* Indeed, before **any** human sin was ever committed God warned us of its deadly consequences. *And the Lord God commanded the man, "You are free to eat from any tree* *in the garden; but you must not eat from the tree of the knowledge of good and evil, for when you eat of it you will surely die" (Genesis 2:16-17).*

Sin is a killer! Jesus Himself characterized it so well when He said, *the thief comes only to steal and kill and destroy.*[1] Our generation would be wise to take a hard look at what the Bible teaches us about sin and its nature. God said sin desires to have us. We must realize sin is actively aggressively pursuing our young people. Sin is surely crouching at the door of this generation; it desires to have them! Apart from the grace of God, once sin gets its hooks in them, it will begin to pull them inescapably down to destruction.

I often hear Christians say there has always been sin and evil, it is no worse now than ever. While I agree that sin and evil has always been present, I believe that in any given society some generations deal with temptations unheard of in previous ones. Jesus Himself predicted in the last days, *Because of the increase of wickedness, the love of most will grow cold...* And in this same passage He indicated because of this *many would turn away from the faith.*[2]

Paul certainly echoes this sentiment in 2 Timothy 3:1-5: *But mark this: There will be terrible times in the last days. People will be lovers of themselves, lovers of money, boastful, proud, abusive, disobedient to their parents, ungrateful, unholy, without love, unforgiving, slanderous, without self-control, brutal, not lovers of the good, treacherous, rash, conceited, lovers of pleasure rather than lovers of God—having a form of godliness but denying its power. Have nothing to do with them.*

Notice also in Paul's warning that the younger generation is not immune to that evil age. The phrase, *disobedient to their parents*, obviously means that even the young will be dealing with all the attitudes and temptations in that time. Whether we are truly in the season described as *the last days*, by both the Lord Jesus and Paul, could be debated. However, these scriptures certainly make the case that evil's influence can increase in any given generation. In our day and time, I cannot help but see all the immoral behavior that both Jesus and Paul described, especially when I am on college campuses.

Kids today face a host of dangerous temptations that would have been unheard of in any other generation. The internet demonstrates this more clearly than any other. Researchers recently revealed that kids between the ages of ten and seventeen are regularly exposed to online pornography. Forty-two percent of kids in this age bracket said they had seen images of people naked or having sex in the past twelve months.[3] Psychiatrists tell us kids this age are now seeing things they are not emotionally prepared to see. Not only does the internet put them at serious risk of bringing them in contact with sexual predators, exposure to graphic sexual images likely leads kids to become sexually active too soon.

Many kids in the internet generation think all this graphic sexual imagery is no big deal and most admit they seek out X-rated material. As I speak to young people today, I am absolutely convinced they are completely **in the dark** about sin's real face and the deadly payday it brings. Paul wrote *the wages of sin is death!* [4]

Unfortunately, most of the kids I speak with scoff at the idea of sin. Sadly, this includes many kids who grew up in church. They seem to love to defend and even flaunt behaviors that the Bible condemns.

Today, less than ten percent of young people who consider themselves born again still believe in moral absolutes. Indeed, even **61%** of "Christian" teens who *claim to have a meaningful relationship with Jesus, believe premarital sex __IS NOT__ morally wrong*.[5] The shift in thinking this represents is virtually incalculable. I was not raised in church, and was a teenager in the seventies and a terrible sinner. But not on my darkest day would I have denied that sex outside of marriage was wrong. Most of my peers felt the same way. I know because we would talk about it. Although most of us chose not to live by it, we still had a sense of right and wrong. We still had a conscience to answer to, and we knew certain things were definitely wrong. We not only knew premarital sex was wrong, it was considered a **BIG** sin, if not the biggest. Now, even the majority of kids who have been raised in church and consider themselves Christians, think there is nothing wrong with sex outside of marriage. This is but one example.

A Dangerous Shift—The Disease Has Spread

When cancer is discovered in someone, their chance of survival depends largely on if it has been detected early. In other words, if it is somewhat isolated to one very specific part of the body, it is easier to cure and there is hope. However, if it has spread to many organs or systems, then naturally this presents a more monumental challenge.

The Bible speaks of sin and tells us it has a similar progression. It is one thing to sin and to instantly know and acknowledge the *wrongness* of that act. To still have a tender conscience toward God offers great hope. But it is quite another thing to sin and then harden your heart, and say, "I'm not interested in what God says. In fact, **I** state, there is nothing wrong with my behavior." That sin has progressed and spread all the way into the belief system, their attitude toward it is vastly different. First of all, it is dangerous because they will seek no cure for the disease. They will reject the medicine of God's conviction.

Secondly, as I have already said, to persist in that behavior will require a person to harden their heart against God, and that is more dangerous than we can fathom. If we let sin determine our belief system, instead of God's Word, we're letting that deadly disease spread to the core of our soul. Once this happens, it will run unchecked and spread to every area of our life. We will effectively be cutting ourselves off from God. The scripture says, *If I had cherished sin in my heart, the Lord would not have listened (Psalm 66:18).* The Prophet Isaiah said, *Your iniquities have separated you from your God (Isaiah 59:2a).*

It is obvious we are losing a generation when only a third of *churched* teens say that they believe in Jesus as the Son of God and plan to continue attending church once they leave home. Sadly, it seems even the majority who claim to believe in Jesus simply have no conviction that they should live any different than teens who do not believe in Jesus. In other words, their worldview and ethics are in no way Christ-like. In things like lying, cheating, sexual activity, and harming others, they are almost identical to kids who do not have a professed Christian belief system.

This is what I find so terrifying! We are not simply talking about teenagers *sowing their wild oats*; all generations do that. There is something much, much more permanent to this.

Today, young people are completely throwing away Christianity's belief system and buying into the world's convoluted beliefs. Even the ones raised in church by Christian parents, who consider themselves born again believers in Jesus, are able to sin seemingly without remorse. In other words, they just don't buy into what Christianity is all about, which is following after Jesus and living a life modeled after the Word of God.

Our kids now are not sinning simply because their flesh is weak, they are living in sin because of their belief system. They simply do not accept the Bible as their moral guide. Again, we recognize this is the crafty serpent's original lie from Eden. Look at the first four words Satan ever uttered on planet earth, **"Did God really say…?"**

He doesn't start with a bold statement; he is too smart for that. No, he starts with a subtle question, *Did God really say?* A little seedling of doubt about the validity and trustworthiness of God planted in the soil of the heart. After tempting Eve with the forbidden fruit in verse four, he offered her this assurance about her sin, *You will not surely die.*[6] "You don't have to do what God said, there will be no consequence." Same evil lies, just a new generation.

Just like Adam and Eve in the garden, this beguiled generation does not believe they will pay a price for disobeying God. But they are wrong—dead wrong. James, the half brother of Jesus, tells us what happens when sin is allowed to run its full course and exactly who is to blame. *When tempted, no one should say, "God is tempting me." For God cannot be tempted by evil, nor does he tempt anyone; but each one is tempted when, by his own evil desire, he is dragged away and enticed. Then, after desire has conceived, it gives birth to sin; and sin, when it is full-grown, gives birth to death (James 1:13-15).*

The Language of Blasphemy

As I have spent countless hours conversing with young people on the quads and food courts of America's college campuses, I have noticed something significant. When people do not believe there will be any consequences or punishment for what they say and do, they recklessly throw away all restraint. Because of that, not only the worldly kids but many of the kids raised in church speak *blasphemy as a native language.* They think it is so cute to say inconceivably profane and insolent things against God. They routinely merge His name with all manner of profanity and sexual vulgarity.

I cannot print anything even close to the things they say so nonchalantly. I often caution them, "Please, please don't say those kinds of things; you have no idea how serious it is!" But it seems to come from some deep-seated hostility toward God; they verbalize it with such relish. However, few things could be more disturbing than their **literal** competition to see who can *out-blaspheme* one another on the internet. Sadly, there is no shortage of participants; thousands of unchurched kids, along with many former church youth group members, take part with the stated purpose of damning their own souls. They very specifically and brazenly cite Jesus' own words in their videos: ***But whoever blasphemes against the Holy Spirit will never be forgiven; he is guilty of an eternal sin (Mark 3:29).*** Then they arrogantly defy God to send them to hell!

My ardent hope is their very ignorance and naiveté will shield them from actually committing the unpardonable sin. However, the fact that this is going on at all should be a chilling indication concerning the depth of resentment taking root in the souls of so many in this generation against God. It is truly heartbreaking to see and hear young people so casually and thoughtlessly insult the Spirit of Grace and trample under foot Jesus, the Son of the Living God.

We have seen time and again that God's Word clearly warns that sin is deadly. I do not sense at all that this generation has ever truly been warned of the consequences of sin. They seem to have little resistance to evil, because they do not believe there will ever be a payday or any real penalty. Too many of them have no idea of the heartache, misery, and pain that inevitably follows disobeying God.

We must somehow begin to build into the foundation of our children the reality that a life of sin and disobedience to God will ultimately bring a horrible result. For those who have either missed out on this foundation or cast it off, my hope is to strategically be one last safety barricade of God's grace. God has called me to stand in the free speech zones of universities and present the alternative point-of-view on spiritual matters. I want to be a flashing warning sign of danger ahead, an impediment on the broad road that leads to destruction. I warn these impressionable young people of the folly, regret, and danger that will follow a decision to reject Jesus and pursue a life of sin.

Rescue those being led away to death; hold back those staggering toward slaughter. Proverbs 24:11

Chapter 10

A Pastor's Daughter Throws Jesus Away at College

M y wife and I sat waiting for the mid-day class break at the *University of North Carolina at Chapel Hill.* I felt a little nervous because this was my first time to preach this school year. The free speech zone at this very liberal college is a large depression about three feet deep fashioned in red brick pavers, and is appropriately called *The Pit.* This day there were several tables set up at the center by the *Gay and Lesbian Student Association.* They were passing out condoms and literature promoting their lifestyle and selling tickets to a *drag fashion show.* Hundreds of students were already milling about, eating fast-food, laughing, and hanging out.

Soon the class break came and thousands of students began pouring into the area. I knew it was time to go to work. Becky gave me an encouraging smile and I walked across *The Pit* to my favorite preaching spot. I said one last prayer, squeezed my Bible, lifted up my voice above the normal everyday polite level, and started talking about Jesus! Thankfully, in only a couple of minutes I had drawn a nice crowd of fifteen or twenty by speaking on the issue of Evolution vs. Intelligent Design. The students started engaging and throwing out questions.

It is so trendy to reject Christ in today's college culture. From the classroom to dorm room, enormous pressure comes to bear on anyone holding to the *archaic old superstition* called Christianity. Many modern-sounding arguments are used to drive a wedge between the hearts of kids raised in church and their parents' *old fashioned beliefs.*

Soon a self-assured young lady, named Allison, came and plopped down on the steps in front of me and began to offer her *views* on Christianity. The following is a brief excerpt from a conversation that lasted close to an hour with a pastor's daughter.

As I have already stated, these kids speak the language of blasphemy. Although I have included no profanity, I have left a couple of her crude statements intact. Her words may be offensive to some, but I leave them in the hope that Christians will be awakened to the real situation and begin to pray as never before for the next generation. I want you to realize as you read that this young lady is not some peculiar exception to the mindset I find on campus these days, her views are the *politically correct* rule. Sadly, she represents the norm and I have talked to so many others just like her.

Allison - First of all I believe that the church should have a political agenda... I believe in using the religion, I guess it's like propaganda... It's the god of my ancestors and because of that I have a cultural tie to religion, but that's where my Christianity stops. Outside of that, all of the kings, disciples, the prophets, they're all men. Your God has a penis; I wouldn't serve God unless she was a woman!

Ken - So what you're saying is, if God sent His Son to bleed and die on a rugged cross, to pay your pardon, your penalty, you would reject that simply because you believe the Bible is a sexiest book?

Allison - Yes, I would. A lot of Christians today try to say, oh well, it really just means a woman submits but a man has to honor his wife and love her as his own body... But still it's very plain.

Ken - It is. I don't know how much you know about management, but in any type of management situation somebody has to make the final decision. For instance, I find you to be extremely easy to talk to. So I'm going to judge you on that basis because I've interacted with you. In a classroom situation, you have professors. Some of them might be men. Now in that situation you have to submit to their authority. That doesn't mean that they are superior to you. They may not be as good a person as you. They've got a guy (professor) in Wisconsin who is a pedophile on staff. So that doesn't mean they are superior to you. In that situation somebody has to be the authority, but that does not devalue you as a person.

Allison - That's fine. But the fact that Christ says because you have a penis, that makes you the head of the household. That makes you the ultimate authority. You are the one that makes the final decisions on everything because you have a penis. I think that's ludicrous!

Ken - First of all, Jesus didn't really characterize it just like that. Secondly, I think you're wrong about the Bible. For one thing Jesus Christ, when He came, elevated women in a world where that was politically incorrect. So basically what you're saying is, that in your opinion, Jesus is ludicrous.

Allison - No, I think that specific scripture (is ludicrous.)

Ken - You just said, *If Jesus said it...*

Allison - Then, yes (he's ludicrous)...The Bible says I am the way the truth and the life and no man comes to the Father but by me. But is it fair...all those other people who have died for a cause and who weren't *saved* quote, unquote—

87

they're just roasted? That's just ludicrous. It seems to me there are many paths to God.

Ken - I just want you to come to grips with your position. You're saying that you're smarter and superior to Jesus Christ.

Allison - No. I'm not saying that.

Ken - You just said it was ludicrous.

Allison - I disagree with that particular scripture. And so I guess that doesn't make me a Christian.

Ken - He died in your place, Allison. He died to take away your punishment.

Allison - Right.

Ken - You don't have to pay for your crimes.

Allison - That's what the good book says.

Ken - So you would reject that based on really what I would call...(Allison interrupts).

Allison - If I have to submit to my husband, yes.

Ken - You would rather go burn in hell forever.

Allison - On that one, I sure as hell would!

Ken - You would?

Allison - I would.

Ken - I don't think you have really thought it through.

Allison - I have.

Ken - No, I don't think it would be worth it.

Allison - Ken, I used to be a Christian.

Ken - Oh, now there's a sad statement.

Allison - (laugh) My father's a minister.

Ken - Oh my gosh. Does he know your position now?

Allison - Yea. He prays and cries every day.

Ken - Well, you'll probably come back now if he's praying for you. Once those dads start praying for you... So you think this issue of sexism...(Allison interrupts).

Allison - Gender equality is very important to me.

Ken - I wouldn't personally gamble my soul on it.

Allison - The flip side of that is I'm supposed to call you my lord and master just as Sarah called Abraham...

Ken - Now where did you get that?

Allison - It's in Genesis.

Ken - Nowhere does the New Testament say my wife is supposed to call me lord and master. I've been married 15 years. Never one time has my wife called me lord and master.

Allison - But I bet in 1850 she probably would have. So then, am I free because Christ has set me free or because we've already had one or two feminist movements where someone challenged the fundamental interpretation of those scriptures? Do I owe my liberation as a woman to those people who challenged scripture or to the scripture itself? Back in the day, you could justify rape, domestic violence... (Ken interrupts).

Ken - No. no.

Allison - There's scripture...

Ken - No.

Allison - Yes, you could.

Ken - There is no scripture in the entire Bible that justifies rape. As a matter of fact, if you read the Law of Moses, that is a capital crime in the Bible.

Allison - No it isn't.

Ken - It is a capital crime in the Bible. I don't know what professor or who told you that. There's no scripture in the Bible that justifies rape. That is a lie.

Allison - Most people would say that now. But 150 years ago they did.

Ken - I could go in that bookstore and buy a UNC blue tee-shirt and go to a convenience store and say, I rob you in the name of UNC. That's no reflection on this university. And what people did 150 years ago or during the crusades, that's no reflection on the person of Jesus Christ. Not at all. It has nothing to do with Him. One thing—you name one thing

Jesus ever said that subjugated women to men. Any word that is in red in the Bible.

Allison - Wait a minute (lengthy pause).

Ken - She's working on it. She's searching the hard drive.

(Allison laughs - lengthy pause)

Allison - Well, it wasn't what he said, it's what he didn't say. It goes back to the cross. The cross is irrelevant for me.

Ken - Do you ever think about how serious that is for you to say that? Let me give you an example. In the early 1900's there was a municipal judge. One day a very sad case came before him. A certain man who was very poor and had always been poor snapped and committed a crime. In a fit of frustration he smashed a store window and stole an item of significant value. He had wanted extra money for his family. But his plan went terribly wrong and he was immediately caught. His case was soon brought before the judge!

The trembling man was sorry and remorseful. He plead guilty and begged the judge for mercy! He wished he hadn't done it. He did not want to pay for his crime. But the judge couldn't simply say, *Oh never mind, the law doesn't matter.* He had the very specific written law; he had sentencing guidelines and parameters. In this case, it was something like a $100 fine or jail time. The judge saw the situation and he did not want it to play out like that. But he had to go by the law. And so as the judge he found him guilty and sentenced him—$100 fine or jail time. He could not set aside law. The judge knew very well this man did not have the money to pay the fine, so it would mean jail time. He knew in this case, this would only further damage the man's life. He would have a criminal record and probably lose his job and family.

So the judge did something extraordinary. He took off his robe, left it lying behind his great desk, adjourned the court briefly, and walked around to where the man stood. He pulled out of his own pocket the $100 and gave it to the man as a gift simply as a fellow human being, not as the judge. He went back up, put on his robe, and reopened the court. Then he said, *$100 fine or jail time. What's it going to be?* The man said, *I'll pay the fine*, and gave him the money. The judge told the man his fine had been paid and he was free to go.

Can you imagine the arrogance if the man had instead thrown the judge's money back in his face, spit on his merciful offer, and then defied him to not throw him in jail? Do you think the judge would be inclined to leave this man unpunished? Now, the implication is obvious. The very God of the universe has sent His Son onto this planet…(Allison interrupts)

Allison - I think that was a very warm and touching story. But…

Ken - But, what? It was based on your remark that the cross is irrelevant. That's what God is going to base your judgment on. You're taking the blood of His Son and literally just walking around on it, completely disrespecting it, spitting on it. You know, Allison, I really do love you.

Allison - And I love you too, Ken

Ken - I care about what happens to you. I think you should go to bed every night thinking about this whole position of rejecting the Son of God for some silly modern political issue. I have hope for you because you've got a praying daddy… (Allison starts to leave for class) I enjoyed talking to you.

Allison - You're a good preacher. You should come more often.

Ken - You should think about these things.

Allison - You're awesome. I really got a lot out of it.

Ken - I'm going to join with your dad and pray for you.

Chapter 11

The Danger of Air Conditioning Hell

The sense of urgency I mentioned earlier in chapter two can only be cultivated when we are willing to genuinely realize what is at stake. I have always believed that telling people about the salvation of Jesus is the most important thing possible. Not long after I got saved, a friend and I used to talk to teenagers every weekend at their local *cruising hang outs*. We passed out hundreds of Gospel tracts a month and talked to kids about Jesus for hours on end in parking lots, parks, and on street corners.

We believed something was truly at stake. We believed they were in danger! When they were particularly rebellious and careless with their souls, we warned them that someday they would face God on Judgment Day to give an account of their life and actions. Sometimes we had the privilege of watching them *sober up,* in a manner of speaking, before our very eyes as God's Spirit convicted them. They would be mocking God insolently one minute and then a few minutes later would be in tears, apologizing for their behavior. It was so sweet to see tears coursing down their cheeks as they prayed to Jesus to forgive them for their sins.

For the most part, the kids I dealt with back then, no matter how naughty they behaved, had a perception that they were *running from God*. They could recognize that and admit they knew they needed to get right with God. They almost all believed in God in their heart of hearts and expressed a need for His forgiveness. Even if at that moment they were not willing to bow to Him, they would acknowledge His authority.

The majority of young people I speak to today are a whole new breed. There does not seem to be anything inside of them willing to acknowledge God's authority. Because of that, I perceive real spiritual danger for them. I am convinced that if they do not turn around, they will lose their eternal souls. But what does that really mean? And how concerned do we really need to be? How we define that concept determines to a large degree how we react to God's Word. For the saint, it will very directly impact their burden for the lost. For the sinner, it will dramatically affect how they respond to God's message of salvation.

I believe this is one of the primary reasons this generation is not buying into Christianity's belief system, and why they are discarding the message of Jesus Christ. Most of them have absolutely no perception that anything is at stake. To them, if they choose to believe or not is simply a matter of choice—like, *What kind of car do you like? What are your spiritual beliefs? What kind of ice cream is your favorite?* There are no real ramifications to choices like these, and they carelessly put belief in Jesus in this same category.

What Lies Beneath?

As I said earlier, if our kids hear no concern in our voice about their spiritual condition, they will take that as affirmation that all is well. They will most likely do the easy thing and follow the crowd and continue in the same direction as the rest of the herd. Jesus characterized this as the **broad road that leads to destruction.**[1] He was seriously trying to get our attention with such a statement! A quick look at the Greek word *apōlĕia,* here translated *destruction,* leaves no doubt of that. In this context it means *eternal spiritual ruin, damnation, perdition*!

To make any substantive difference in the tide of humanity rushing down this broad road to destruction, forces us to grapple with one monumental issue. What is at the end of that road? If they are to be persuaded into making a virtual U-turn on the road of life, we ourselves must be persuaded of something. That is, there is a serious repercussion for those who do not. We must earnestly seek the answer to this question, *What happens to people who lose their souls*? Or as the Apostle Peter expressed it, **What will become of the ungodly and the sinner?** [2]

That is not really a difficult question at all. We know it too instinctively not to instantly think of the answer. But facing that reality is very, very difficult. Most of us have difficulty verbalizing it in a serious conversation in its unvarnished form. We tend to downplay it with less than direct words, or always mix it with some comic relief. If we were to ask most evangelicals, *What happens to people who are not saved?* They would probably respond with something like, *they go down there*, and give a quick downward point. Some might even add a humorous comment about the warm temperature below.

However, I think very few actually allow themselves to contemplate or consider seriously what *losing their soul* will mean for anyone they know and love. The Bible states it, however, in very plain terms that we can all understand. *If anyone's name was not found written in the book of life, he was thrown into the lake of fire (Revelation 20:15).* Our generation, it seems, just cannot bring themselves to think of it in those terms. As I have already stated, what you believe about this subject determines if you have any concern for lost souls.

There are basically two choices when considering the unimaginable reality of hell awaiting those who do not believe the Gospel. The first response is to pray with a gut-wrenching heartfelt passion that your loved ones and friends would turn to God and be saved. This is especially true when we consider our children. The simpler option is to **pretend**, for all intents and purposes, that hell is no longer part of the equation.

It seems to me our generation, for the most part, has chosen the latter, and statistics bear that out. A recent poll found that two thirds (**68%**) of evangelical protestants essentially believe people can obtain salvation another way other than Jesus and still get to heaven.[3] Could it be our kids have lost their convictions because our generation has lost ours?

The world takes note of our loss of conviction and it doesn't make them respect us more; in fact, it makes them scoff. As a writer for *Newsweek* noted, **"Churchgoers take comfort: hell has all but disappeared from modern Christian theology"** [4]

The Bottom Line

It just sounds so much more sophisticated to do away with this seemingly small unpleasant part of Christian theology, but the consequences are truly dire if we do! If we consciously remove or unconsciously ignore this bottom-line of Christian belief, then the entire Gospel collapses. If God's love, mercy, grace, and salvation are like a set of exquisite, fine china, then hell is like the tablecloth underneath. No matter how unattractive we may think it is, it is still down there. And if we think we can simply jerk it out and leave the rest of the Gospel still intact, we are sadly mistaken. Like the fine china, all we have left is shattered, broken, senseless pieces.

What are we then to do with the hundreds of references in scripture to hell, fire, flames, and the ultimate truth that God will indeed punish the wicked? If these are to be considered inaccuracies, then the integrity of the Bible as a whole as God's trustworthy Word is demolished. The entire Gospel then becomes completely senseless. If the sinner will not, in the end be punished for sin, then why does the Bible speak so often about a Day of Judgment? Why does the Bible say, THE PUNISHMENT that brought us peace was upon Jesus? Why was He crushed, pierced, and bruised for our iniquities? [5] Why does the book of Hebrews claim, *without the shedding of blood there is no forgiveness?* [6] If our sins do not need to be forgiven then there will really be no Judgment Day for the UN-forgiven, and Jesus died in vain. The cross would then be truly foolishness.

If there is no hell below, then all of Jesus' words and warnings about that place fall to the ground, as useless empty philosophical prose—lies actually. That would also mean Jesus was not the Savior of the world. If the world doesn't really need to be saved, then who exactly do we believe He was, a mortal prophet? If that is the case, then our entire faith is a farce and we have believed in vain.

Furthermore, if there is no hell then there probably is no heaven, for the same Lord and the same Book promises both. If there is no resurrection, there is no Gospel. As Paul so aptly said it, *For if the dead are not raised, then Christ has not been raised either. And if Christ has not been raised, your faith is futile; you are still in your sins. Then those also who have fallen asleep in Christ are lost. If only for this life we have hope in Christ, we are to be pitied more than all men (1 Corinthians 15:16-19).* If that is the road modern mainstream *christianity* chooses to go down, I refuse to go with them. I think they are wrong, dead wrong in fact. What if hell is still down there? I choose to stay on the narrow road that leads to eternal life with my Lord Jesus!!! And I want to do all I can to help others, especially the youth of America, exit the broad road that leads to destruction.

A Perception of Danger

In the excellent book, *Hell Under Fire,* R. Albert Mohler, Jr. documents this alarming trend within evangelical Christianity to marginalize hell. He astutely points out the truly disastrous unwanted result. *This is no theological trifle. As one observer has asked, "Could it be that the only result of attempts, however well-meaning, to air-condition Hell, is to ensure that more and more people wind up there?"* [7]

I could not agree more. I believe *air-conditioning* hell is a large part of why two-thirds of young people raised in church do not believe Jesus is the Son of God. It is surely the reason about that same number indicate they have no intention of going to church when they leave home. They have not been made aware of the consequences of not believing in Jesus.

There are serious warnings in the Bible for those who reject faith in Jesus. Some of these ominous words are lurking right next to our very favorite verses. I find they are largely ignored today, but we must take note of them. **John 3:16** is the best example. It is unquestionably the most well known verse of scripture in modern America. Even many of the most secularized kids I speak to on college campuses can quote this verse. It is a truly wonderful verse and has been called the Gospel in a nut shell. But I find almost no one knows the four verses that follow it.

For God so loved the world that he gave his one and only Son, that whoever believes in him shall not perish but have eternal life. For God did not send his Son into the world to condemn the world, but to save the world through him. Whoever believes in him is not condemned, but whoever does not believe stands condemned already because he has not believed in the name of God's one and only Son. This is the verdict: Light has come into the world, but men loved darkness instead of light because their deeds were evil. Everyone who does evil hates the light, and will not come into the light for fear that his deeds will be exposed (John 3:16-20).

Yes, it is true God does love the world and sent His only Son to save it! But even embedded in this verse is the criterion for eternal life. We must believe! The overwhelming majority of this generation of American youth does not believe. In that case, stern warnings from the words of Jesus follow. If we love our darkness and evil deeds and do not believe, we are condemned already! If that is too vague, at the end of this passage from the Apostle John's Gospel, John the Baptist declares: *Whoever believes in the Son has eternal life, but whoever rejects the Son will not see life, for God's wrath remains on him (John 3:36).*

Frankly, the fact that Jesus stated people who do not believe stand **condemned** already, and that John the Baptist indicated **God's wrath** remains on **everyone** who rejects the Son, is difficult for most modern evangelicals to swallow. These truths have become so foreign to our ears that even these Biblical terms now seem out of step with Jesus Himself. It is not because they are, He actually **said** them. It is because they have been so neglected in much of the preaching that we hear these days. These concepts, like God's wrath and people being condemned, have the ring of danger. It is this very perception of danger that we have lost.

We also so marginalize the concept of the devil, the enemy of our souls, that he is virtually a non-player in this very real drama. As John Eldridge so eloquently points out in his great message, **The Epic**: *Every story has a villain, because yours does. But most of you don't live like it. Most of you don't live like the story has a villain, and that makes life very confusing.*

Much of the modern church conveniently forgets that we are at war and there is an enemy who ruthlessly kills and destroys lives. There is an enemy whose sole intent is to divert unsuspecting humans from a relationship with their Creator. Once captured, if they are not saved, they will be dragged into hell.

A Voice from Hell and the Grave!

Not only did Jesus speak about people being condemned, He gave us the most vivid description possible of exactly what that will mean. The only message ever brought back from someone experiencing the torments of hell was communicated to us directly from the lips of Jesus. He allowed us the unusual and extraordinary privilege of seeing and hearing the unutterable regret of someone in that place. It is found in Luke, chapter sixteen. Here Jesus tells the story of the life and death of two men, an unrighteous rich man and a poor beggar named Lazarus who was in right-standing with God.

> *There was a rich man who was dressed in purple and fine linen and lived in luxury every day...The time came when the beggar died and the angels carried him to Abraham's side. The rich man also died and was buried. In hell, where he was in torment, he looked up and saw Abraham far away, with Lazarus by his side. So he called to him, "Father Abraham, have pity on me and send Lazarus to dip the tip of his finger in water and cool my tongue, because I am in agony in this fire."*

But Abraham replied, "Son, remember that in your lifetime you received your good things, while Lazarus received bad things, but now he is comforted here and you are in agony. And besides all this, between us and you a great chasm has been fixed, so that those who want to go from here to you cannot, nor can anyone cross over from there to us."

He answered, "Then I beg you, father, send Lazarus to my father's house, for I have five brothers. Let him warn them, so that they will not also come to this place of torment." Abraham replied, "They have Moses and the Prophets; let them listen to them." "No, father Abraham," he said, "but if someone from the dead goes to them, they will repent." He said to him, "If they do not listen to Moses and the Prophets, they will not be convinced even if someone rises from the dead"
(Luke 16:19,22-31).

Note first, that Jesus treats this as an account of an actual event, not a parable. In absolutely no instance did Jesus ever use personal names in a parable. However, in this account, He tells us the name of the beggar, Lazarus, as well as referring to by name the real Old Testament person of Abraham. Notice the unmistakable reality captured in the rich man's own words, hell is a place of *torment and flames*. This is an eyewitness account, not a hypothetical theological construct. Secondly, notice that this man was fully cognizant of his own situation. He was not annihilated; he was fully experiencing and regretting his punishment. Thirdly, and most importantly for our context, the rich man desperately desired someone to warn his unsaved loved ones!

At first it may seem ironic that this concern for lost souls comes to us from a sinner confined to hell, but actually it makes perfect sense. Who better to realize that sinners need to be warned about the consequences of the unimaginable tragedy of losing their souls? However Abraham's counsel serves to make us all aware of God's preferred method of saving lost people from this awful place—the proclamation of His Word: *They have Moses and the Prophets; let them listen to them!*

What if people **do** still lose their souls? What if hell is still down there? What if it never really went away? Then it is incumbent upon us to make sure people understand the matchless gift of God's grace and the inherent dangers of rejecting it. For a great many reasons it seems that the exposure our young people are getting to Christianity isn't taking most of them beyond mom and dad's front door. The day they leave youth group for the last time and head off to college is the day too many of them carelessly step off into a deep ocean of spiritual decay. They may tread water for a while, but they soon sink below the dark surface of unbelief. So what happens to those who so quickly turn their back on their faith once they leave home? Did they really ever have a faith?

In a generation where the pressure is relentless and enormous to turn your back on Jesus once you leave home, we must examine what we believe about that. In a culture where it is trendy to pick and choose your spiritual beliefs, we must make sure we are in fact making committed disciples of Jesus Christ; not just getting kids involved in a really cool youth group. We must face these issues head-on and start instilling beliefs in our younger generation that causes them to fall in love with the Lord Jesus, and gets them all the way to heaven's golden streets.

Grace to all who love our Lord Jesus Christ with an <u>undying</u> love. Ephesians 6:24 (Emphasis added)

Chapter 12

A Tale of Two Churches and One Confused Teenager

When I was about twelve years old, one Saturday night my mom informed me that the next day was Mother's Day and I would have to go to church with my grandmother the following evening. Growing up, we did not go to church a lot, so I really didn't want to go. In my rebellious young mind I thought, "She's your mother, why don't you go?" But that is not the kind of thing we said out loud at our house to our mom. So I was going, no matter what. Frankly, I was a little scared because my grandma's church was *old time Pentecostal*. We had heard a lot of wild stories and it was no secret to us just how *lively* their services tended to get. I felt like the *sacrificial mother's day lamb* for our family. Mom took me to my grandparent's house, and they took me to church that Sunday evening.

We sat near the back of the small wood-frame church. I felt relatively safe since everything seemed to be going on at the front of the long narrow sanctuary. We sang a while from the hymn books, which always confused me because I could never figure out how to follow those verses. Then the pastor preached a while. I don't remember hearing a single word of his message. I know I was not misbehaving, that would not have been permitted. Apparently, I wasn't paying any attention so I cannot claim to be guiltless in the matter.

They started singing again but I knew enough about their services to know we were **not** coming to a close. We were just getting started. People started raising their hands, shouting, and running around the church. My grandparents didn't run around though, they stayed in the pew. I just stuck close to them and tried to be invisible, which was getting harder and harder to do. Their style of worship was very participatory, so sure enough, after half an hour I could no longer hide.

The pastor came all the way to the pew where I was sitting—right side, second from the back—and said, "Son, its time you come down to the front and get saved." He took me firmly by my skinny little arm and gave me a gentle tug in the right direction. I had no idea on earth what I was supposed to say, but it was clear to me that "Yes sir" was the only right answer. He ushered me to the front altar and a group of five or six adults gathered around me, praying fervently. The minister told me to bow my head and say a certain prayer. I complied.

He then announced to the congregation that I had just gotten saved, and they really started shouting. They got my hands in the air too and led me around the church aisles for what seemed like a long time. Finally, they returned me to my grandparent's side. My grandmother was really *rejoicing* about my decision. My grandpa was a quiet man and didn't say much.

We got in the car and they took me home. Grandma walked me to the door and told my mom that I had gotten *saved*. I think my mom had a sense of what had happened, so when they left she told me I had to *live it*. I didn't understand that either really. That was the end of this story. I didn't read the Bible. I didn't pray. I didn't start going to church.

Nothing really changed at all. I certainly do not want to disparage my grandmother's faith or *old-time Pentecostals* in general; this was simply my experience as a young boy. In fact, I have enormous respect for my grandmother and will share another story about her remarkable faith in a later chapter.

I became a full-blown teenager over the next couple of years and pursued absolutely nothing godly at all. The truth is, I did just the opposite. As a young man most of my family and friends would have said I was a *good kid*, but I was really living a sinful life. I constantly blasphemed God and did a lot of shameful things. I was completely uncommitted to God. Then one night, when I was about fourteen, I was invited by a friend to a church service. I went out of a sense of obligation to my friend.

This was a youth revival at a Baptist church, and there was an evangelist preaching. He was interesting and funny, but his message became very serious and I heard every word. That night he quoted Jesus from the Book of Revelation. He said, *I know your works, that you are neither cold nor hot. I could wish you were cold or hot. So then, because you are lukewarm, and neither cold nor hot, I will vomit you out of My mouth (Revelation 3:15-16 NKJV).*

You can fool people, but you cannot fool God. I knew lukewarm was the very best description I could have hoped for, and that obviously was not going to cut it with God. I felt the conviction of the Holy Spirit and I knew that I needed to respond somehow. I was guilty of being uncommitted to God and the end result he had indicated, being spewed out of the mouth of Jesus, shook me to the core of my soul. When the evangelist gave the invitation, I went forward that night to the altar.

They lead us all to a room where another man came and asked why I had come. I told him I was afraid I would not go to heaven. He asked if I had ever prayed to receive Christ. I said I wasn't sure, but I told him about praying at grandma's church. He said, "Well you're **OK** then. You just need assurance." I really didn't know what to think. I remember not really feeling very *assured* by the time I went home, but for a few days I really tried to take comfort in his words, "You're OK."

However, nothing changed. I didn't read the Bible, I didn't pray, I didn't start going to church, and I sure didn't turn from my sin. In fact, I got a job at fifteen years old at a local amusement park. It was a terribly evil equation— fifteen hundred teenage boys plus about the same number of teenage girls, equaled lots of sin. The only thing different was that those words of Jesus sometimes haunted me. I was sure I was still in the lukewarm category, if not worse. I was certain I would get spewed out of His mouth on Judgment Day. I almost drowned that next summer while swimming in the Olympic-size employee swimming pool at our amusement park. That was just too close. I'm so thankful God didn't let me die that day. I tremble to think of what would have happened. I absolutely do not think I would have gone to heaven.

One thing is for sure, in no way was I a follower of Jesus in any sense of the word. It would be several more years before I would get saved. At the very least, my experience should help us realize we need to use wisdom when we deal with those who come to respond to God's Word.

Shipwrecked Faith and Other Prickly Issues

Holding on to faith and a good conscience. Some have rejected these and so have shipwrecked their faith (1 Timothy 1:19).

Here Paul talks about people holding on to their faith and then gives an apparent example of someone who does not; in fact, he clearly indicates that they **reject** it instead. He says their faith has been shipwrecked. If salvation can be compared to getting in a ship, I'm convinced I was never really in the boat after my early experiences at church. I don't think it could be said my faith was shipwrecked. I just didn't yet have **a faith** to actually wreck. But what about people who do seem to have a faith that gets wrecked? Or can we know who is really in the ship in the first place?

The subject of huge numbers of young people losing their souls, including a great many of whom have been raised in church, inevitably brings us to the prickly doctrinal issue of eternal security. My desire is that Christians from many creeds and denominations will read this book, including those who hold to the doctrine of eternal security or as some call it *once saved always saved.* I was saved in a Baptist church myself at 17 years old. However, my evangelistic ministry has opened doors for me to preach in many different kinds of churches. This coupled with my personal experience as a confused teenager has caused me to examine this theological question closely.

More than anything else though, the fact that I have spent years talking to people outside the walls of the church about their eternal salvation, has forced me to deal with this subject in an especially practical sense. Many I speak to, particularly in America, have come from a background in church. When I'm out in ministry, I speak almost daily to people who are living truly debauched lifestyles. They are often involved in sexual sin, drunkenness, blaspheming, and using God's name in vain. They generally demonstrate no real interest in God whatsoever.

When the subject of their eternal salvation gets on the table, suddenly, because of a church background, they remember some experience from their childhood. It very often amounted to nothing more than *walking a church aisle* or *shaking a preacher's hand*, but others have actually been baptized or even said the *sinner's prayer*. Naturally, many simply want to use these early experiences as a smokescreen to avoid the *God* subject.

So, as I am speaking to this person about their salvation, what I care about in the most practical terms is, *are they truly right with God?* Personally, I have always been uncomfortable giving someone *assurance* of their salvation if **they** feel unsure. I err toward caution. I think it is far safer to tell them they need to turn from sin and to God. I certainly do not want to be guilty of giving them false assurance based on some experience they may or may not have had many years ago.

I truly have no real desire to debate this issue with Christians to convince them one way or the other. I am an evangelist, not a theologian. I feel my time is far better spent telling lost people how to get saved. However, for the purpose of this book, I consulted three Baptist professors, each with doctorates from seminary. I asked them what the Baptist position would be on this group of close to 90% of young people who leave the faith so quickly after leaving home.

I was truly surprised by their answer. I thought they might say, *Well, even though they have left the faith, their salvation is secure; they will still go to heaven when they die.* None said this. Instead they all said the same thing: that the doctrine of eternal security includes the concept of *the perseverance of the saints.* In other words, a person who is truly saved will continue on with Jesus. They each came to the conclusion that those who so easily fall away at college had never in fact experienced what they called *salvific faith.* In plain terms, *faith that saves.*

Again, I prefer caution. I would much rather exhort a person to get right with God than to offer them a false assurance. A pastor or youth pastor more likely has to deal with a new believer whose heart is truly inclined toward God, but who is struggling to overcome old habits. That is a different scenario. More often than not, I deal with people with no tangible desire to leave their sin or follow Christ.

So, when I encounter a young person under conviction, sensing they are not right with God, I do not try and figure out if they are making a *first time decision* or if they are *re-dedicating* their life. I have no time to pursue a hairsplitting theological discussion, especially with someone who has no clue about such matters. The real issue is not so much the theological argument for or against eternal security. The real issue **is**, *has a person ever truly been saved*! I'm convinced that eternal security is not the doctrine we should be examining so carefully with this generation, but rather the subject of true and false conversion.

Paul said, ***Examine yourselves to see whether you are in the faith; test yourselves. Do you not realize that Christ Jesus is in you—unless, of course, you fail the test? (2 Corinthians 13:5).*** We would be far better served to pass on this piece of wise counsel. They must examine themselves to see whether they are truly in the faith.

Another interesting New Testament exhortation that gives us a very real sense of which attitude is healthy in this process, and the priority it deserves, comes to us from the book of Philippians. Here the Apostle Paul not only counsels people to make sure they are *saved*, rather than just assuming they are, he shows us the gravity with which God expects us to pursue this assurance. ***Continue to work out your salvation with fear and trembling (Philippians 2:12b).***

My main point here is if we are depending on this prominent doctrine of eternal security in regard to this generation, we are making a grave mistake. We dare not think they are *safe*. Two-thirds of our church kids have declared they do not believe the Gospel, they do not believe Jesus is the Son of God. That is the barest minimum prerequisite, by any interpretation, for saving faith—**that we believe**!

In Romans, chapter ten, we are told that part of a genuine confession of salvation specifically involves the confession with your mouth, *Jesus is Lord.* It makes absolutely no sense to believe that God accepts *lip service* as someone turns from their old life and comes to Him. They must truly believe and be acting on the idea that Jesus really is Lord! This is the truest criterion for knowing whether someone is really saved. Is Jesus truly their Lord? The Greek word for Lord, *Kurios,* leaves us with little doubt as to the exact nature of our *post salvation* relationship to Christ. It means *master, owner, possessor.* Jesus is called this 618 times in the New Testament.

Jesus Himself could not have made this clearer when He said, *Why do you call me "Lord, Lord," and do not do what I say? (Luke 6:46).* The Lord Jesus' warning on this subject should be enough to make anyone examine himself to see if they truly are in the faith. He describes a shocking scenario on Judgment Day. *Not everyone who says to me, "Lord, Lord", will enter the kingdom of heaven, but only he who does the will of my Father who is in heaven. Many will say to me on that day, "Lord, Lord did we not prophesy in your name, and in your name drive out demons and perform many miracles?" Then I will tell them plainly, "I never knew you. Away from me, you evildoers!" (Matthew 7:21-23).* No wonder Paul said to work out your salvation with fear and trembling. I have concluded there must be a genuine Lordship involved in saving faith! Sadly, it seems most of the Millennial Generation, including the majority of those raised in church, seem unwilling to bow their knee before the King of kings, Jesus Christ!

What About the Prodigal Son?

As I have written this part of the book, I have been keenly aware of the story of the Prodigal Son found in Luke, chapter fifteen. It is truly one of the most tender examples of the Father's great love for the lost. But in this context, let me make just a couple of observations. This is, of course, the well-known story of a young man who leaves his father's house and pursues a life of sin and self-indulgence. The father lovingly waits for him to return. When the son does return, he is smothered with the father's love and reinstated completely in his favor.

If we want to cling to this in regard to this generation of young people, we must note three things. First, the son inwardly repents and is sorrowful for his behavior. He comes to himself and says internally, and to his father upon his return, *I have sinned against heaven and against you. I am no longer worthy to be called your son.* Secondly, he comes home! He returns to his father's house. Thirdly, the father himself reveals the reason for his jubilant celebration upon his son's return. He regarded his lost condition with the utmost seriousness. He said to his other son, *This brother of yours was dead, and is alive again; he was lost and is found.*

We simply cannot, at this stage, afford to minimize the spiritual danger that surrounds the young people of this generation!

The vast majority of them have never heard the truth of God's Word. Even the greater majority of those raised in church are leaving the Father's house upon graduation from high school and youth group, **85-94%** by most estimates. Even if they could be categorized as prodigals, which is somewhat doubtful considering they do not believe in Jesus Christ, they are still not returning to the Father's house. They remain in the perilous condition described in the story as *dead* and *lost*. There is no evidence at this point to suggest that they are ever returning to church or to belief in Jesus.

No matter your position on eternal security, I cannot imagine any genuine Christian not being able to recognize the utter tragedy of a young person backslidden, living a life of destructive sin, and in rebellion to the Lord Jesus Christ. Nothing good can come from this, so we must be in the business of doing all we can to bring them home.

> *Brethren, if anyone among you wanders from the truth, and someone turns him back, let him know that he who turns a sinner from the error of his way will save a soul from death and cover a multitude of sins. James 5:19-20 (NKJV)*

Chapter 13

A Call to Care

If we do not really believe anything is at stake and if we do not really believe someone will wind up in the place the Bible describes as hell, we can remain indifferent. We will do little or nothing to change their direction. As churches and as individuals, the first and most devastating result will be to lessen, if not remove all together, our urgent concern for the lost. We must realize this will eventually affect our children.

If they are away from God or living in sin, and they see no concern in **our** demeanor, they also will feel no concern. If we lose our sense of urgency about their spiritual well-being, who will pray for them? Who will make the effort to reconcile them to God?

More than anything else, this book is a call to care and to care deeply about the fate of young people all around us! It is a call for every pastor, parent, grandparent, youth worker and Christian to take a realistic look at what is happening to a generation of young people who are being swept away and to ask God what we can do to change this trend. It is a call to pray, to change the way we do business, if necessary. It is a call to take a serious look at the way we present the Gospel, to do all we can to rescue young people from spiritual destruction.

Perhaps some might accuse me of shameful manipulation and playing on emotion in suggesting that young people are losing their souls. They might suggest this notion of people losing their eternal souls is unreal or anecdotal. However, if the Bible is the Word of God, I believe just the opposite is true! We have been lulled to sleep while a generation of young people is, in fact, losing their eternal souls. They **are** being lost forever, never to be found! Far too many of us are being completely unemotional and even blasé about it.

God has always called His people to care and to care deeply when physical or spiritual danger looms on the horizon. Humanity is the apple of His very eye and He cares more than we can imagine. The God of scripture very often alerts His people when they are under a serious threat. In the first chapter of this book, I quoted from the book of Joel, *multitudes in the valley of decision*. It is amazing how closely our day and age mirrors the situation in which this Old Testament prophet found himself.

God revealed to Joel that a terrible day of danger and calamity was fast approaching. Israel was far from God and had pushed Him and His influences out of their lives and society. They had disregarded His laws and embraced every possible immorality. Now sin's inevitable consequence, God's judgment, was bearing down directly on them and was poised to sweep over them like a tsunami. In the first few verses of chapter two, God warns them that *a day of darkness and gloom, and a day of clouds and blackness was close at hand.*

But **was it** inevitable? Was there still hope to forestall the consequences of transgressions? Just before the dreadful events God had described were about to be set in motion, He gave them this word of hope. *"Even now," declares the*

Lord, "return to me with all your heart, with fasting and weeping and mourning." Rend your heart and not your garments. Return to the Lord your God, for he is gracious and compassionate, slow to anger and abounding in love, and he relents from sending calamity. Who knows? He may turn and have pity and leave behind a blessing (Joel 2:12-14a Emphasis added).

Notice the phrase, *Even now!* Despite the wickedness of the times, despite being on the very brink of judgment, God was ready to offer a last reprieve of mercy. He is always ready to forgive because of His beautiful nature. For truly He is gracious and compassionate, slow to anger, abounding in love. We will visit this subject of His disposition and character later in depth; it is our hope. For now, however, we cannot miss the important prerequisite of the fulfillment of that tender offer. God expected His people to return to Him with all their hearts and to fully recognize the gravity of the situation. They were to do this by fasting, weeping, and mourning over the current state of affairs.

Extreme Measures!

Only when God's people rightly perceive the unimaginable tragedy of multitudes losing their eternal souls will they respond to His wake-up call. Only when we realize the failure of the status quo will we suspend the business as usual approach. Then and only then will we get serious about calling out to God to turn a generation around before it is too late. God's expectation of how seriously we should approach this kind of spiritual warfare is crystal clear from His instructions to Joel's generation:

Blow the trumpet in Zion, declare a holy fast, call a sacred assembly. Gather the people, consecrate the assembly; bring together the elders, gather the chil-

dren, those nursing at the breast. Let the bridegroom leave his room and the bride her chamber. Let the priests, who minister before the Lord, weep between the temple porch and the altar. Let them say, "Spare your people, O Lord. Do not make your inheritance an object of scorn, a byword among the nations. Why should they say among the peoples, 'Where is their God?'" Then the Lord will be jealous for his land and take pity on his people (Joel 2:15-18).

We live in a refined, civil society where we have *disturbing the peace* statutes in place to maintain a certain level of serenity. Even so, sometimes those norms do not apply. Has your calm ever been shattered by the ear-splitting wail of a passing emergency vehicle siren? Have you ever been jolted to attention by the reverberating moan of an outdoor storm warning? Or perhaps heard the irritating loud buzz of the emergency broadcast system interrupting your radio or television broadcast?

My wife and I live in what is known as *tornado ally*, so we have a great appreciation for the concept of WARNINGS. We always take it serious when a storm warning is issued. We recently attended a mission's conference in another town here in Texas. Shortly after entering our hotel room I noticed a placard on the back of our door with the rather disturbing image of a tornado, with this announcement: *The office of emergency management and this establishment are concerned for your safety. As a result, the city has installed an outdoor early warning system to notify the public in the event of a tornado or other emergency. If you hear an outdoor siren, please take the following precautions...*

They were warning us ahead of time in case of an emergency that the rules of normal genteel quietness would be suspended. Why do we tolerate such disturbing sounds in our otherwise noise-protected environment? Because we understand that at that moment an individual or even a whole community is in grave danger, and we all recognize their well-being is more important than our momentary tranquility.

This is the exact approach God prescribes in this situation—***Blow the trumpet,*** He commands! This is God's emergency warning system when spiritual peril approaches His people. I believe in our day just such a situation is at hand with the crisis of faith among our young people and we dare not ignore God's warning. We must obey Him, put the trumpet to our lips, and sound the alarm in America!

This is an Emergency!

Notice also the nature of God's call to all His people—no one is exempt. It is a resounding *all hands on deck* plea to rescue the perishing. Gather the people, elders, teens, young mothers, ministers; even a honeymooning couple is not excused from the sacred assembly (verses 16-17). And all for what purpose? Simply to intercede before God for those in danger: ***Spare your people, O Lord.***

While a great many churches have gotten away from the practice of holding revivals, this is exactly what is needed today. We need to respond to God's call for sacred assembly. We need to pull ourselves away from the world and its influence and consecrate ourselves fresh and new to God. We need to carve out time away from our busy schedules and secular entertainment and begin to intercede for this generation of young people. We need to be calling out like Joel's generation, ***Spare your people, O Lord!***

Just as in Joel's situation, we have to recognize the urgent nature of what is befalling this generation and suspend normal operation. We must jettison every trivial pursuit and run to the lifeboats, for the alarm has been sounded! Not only does Joel's small book tell us to sound the alarm and pull everyone together for rescue operations, it even indicates what degree of emotion is appropriate. *Let the priests, who minister before the Lord, weep between the temple porch and the altar.* I cannot remember the last time I saw a preacher actually weep while declaring the Gospel. I know it has been at least a decade. That is too much out of vogue for today's sophisticated mindset. Generally, any time I have heard a modern pastor refer to someone shedding tears in the pulpit, it is in a negative context—something to be mocked or ridiculed.

It would seem such raw emotion is out of step with modern *churchdom*. Instead the approach in much of the church world these days is more corporate in nature and style than Biblical. Therefore, very few in this generation have ever heard an impassioned plea to turn from sin and to God in heartfelt repentance. Our results speak for themselves. We are losing the Millennial Generation and have been for quite some time now. We must return to a Christianity that carries some weight and authority, that properly conveys the true gravity of people losing their souls. Preachers must awake and throw off the apathy that has paralyzed our age. We must cast aside dignity and restraint, and preach and plead with a force equal to the tragic result of people losing their souls.

Although it may currently be out of vogue, it is not difficult to find such powerful Christianity. If you thoughtfully look back through the pages of church history, you will easily note that we have lost much fervency in the way we present the Gospel. Today we don't look all that different to the church in England in the early eighteenth century. Christianity had become a polite, unemotional affair, with fashionable, sensitive, user-friendly services. The preaching style of most ministers of that day has been described as controlled, dignified, and even stuffy. No intense emotional appeals were made for sinners to repent, and just like us, the Anglican Church was **also** losing a generation. The masses felt little need for what the church offered, until a young man named George Whitefield stormed onto the scene.

This great English open-air preacher had a preaching style that was described as intense, emotional, dramatic and with the *unreserved use of tears.* He once said, **"You blame me for weeping, but how can I help it when you will not weep for yourselves, though your immortal souls are on the verge of destruction."** He approached Christianity as it should be, as a life and death struggle for the souls of mankind. He preached 18,000 messages in his life, to approximately ten million hearers. His preaching not only rocked England and Scotland, his open-air preaching tour of 1739 sparked what is now called America's Great Awakening. Immortal souls are also on the verge of destruction in our generation; we too should be weeping.

The prince of preachers, Charles Spurgeon, also had a passionate ministry philosophy when it came to reaching the lost. He said, **"If sinners will be damned, at least let them leap to hell over our bodies. And if they will perish, let them perish with our arms about their knees, imploring them to stay... Let not one go there unwarned and unprayed for."** How desperately this generation needs church leaders, like Spurgeon, who comprehend the dire spiritual peril of our situation today. We need preachers who are not afraid to stir God's people by articulating the unpleasant reality that lost people are dying and going to hell. I am convinced that it will take nothing less to actually wake us up and turn this generation around.

What is abundantly clear when you read the writings and accounts of church history's greatest soul winners is they cared deeply about the plight of the lost. I certainly do not mean to imply that no one cares today. However, the urgency of the situation demands that we raise the bar and begin to match the emotional intensity of past generations in the way we pray and in the way we present the Gospel. Our casual laid-back approach is not getting the attention of this generation of kids. We would do well to look at the Word of God as our example of an appropriate emotional level as we form our ministry philosophies. If we could return to a level of passion and commitment anything like that of the early church, that would be called revival and it is what we so desperately need.

When the Apostle Paul met with the Ephesian church elders upon his final departure from them, he characterized the exact nature of his ministry style. His opening sentence clearly demonstrates the emotional passion with which he conducted his ministry among them. ***When they arrived, he said to them: "You know how I lived the whole time I was with you, from the first day I came into the province of Asia. I served the Lord with great humility and with tears. (Acts 20:18-19a Emphasis added).*** And his closing statements reveal when it came to their spiritual well-being, in three years of ministry he **lost** none of his emotional intensity. ***So be on your guard! Remember that for three years I never stopped warning each of you night and day with tears (Acts 20:31 Emphasis added).***

Lord, Make Me a Beggar!

One of the most life-changing encounters with God's Word that I have ever experienced came when I was a very young preacher. I was working full-time, attending Bible College, serving as a youth pastor at a local church, and just beginning evangelistic ministry. Every Saturday a few members of my church went out door-to-door to tell people about Jesus. This was a real stretch for me because I am by nature very shy. The thought of ringing someone's door bell and then launching from a cold start into a conversation about the Gospel petrified me. One Saturday morning I was praying and trying to summon the needed courage for the day's outreach. I opened my Bible to a passage that forever changed the way I thought about presenting the Gospel.

All these new things are from God who brought us back to himself through what Christ Jesus did. And God has given us the privilege of urging everyone to come into his favor and be reconciled to him. For God was in Christ, restoring the world to himself, no longer counting men's sins against them but blotting them out. This is the wonderful message he has given us to tell others. We are Christ's ambassadors. God is using us to speak to you: we beg you, as though Christ himself were here pleading with you, receive the love he offers you—be reconciled to God (2 Corinthians 5:18-20 Living Bible).

First of all, I realized that it was a privilege to be entrusted by God with such a glorious message as the Gospel. Secondly, it forever defined for me the exact nature of that message, reconciliation with God. But thirdly, it showed me the depth of emotional dedication and commitment expected of me as an ambassador of Christ. When I read those words of Paul saying, *we beg you as if the Lord Jesus Himself were here pleading with you to receive the love he offers*, I was nothing less than awestruck. I imagined the living Lord Jesus imploring sinners to come to Him. A prayer formed in my heart and mind and escaped out of my mouth before I could reconsider the ramifications.

Lord, make me a beggar, I said. Lord make me so aware of people's lost condition, their deplorable end result, their overwhelming need for a Savior, that I would beg them, if necessary, to be saved. If what it takes to wake them up from their destructive, spiritual stupor is for me to depart from the polite status quo, then so be it. If I have to lose my dignity and my sense of personal pride, then so be it. If I have to get on my knees and beg them to listen, then I will trust You to give me the grace to do that. I realized then and there telling someone about Jesus is not like marketing a new car. It is not simply a matter of telling them His good points, and asking them to sign on the bottom line. To actually reach someone's heart is a life and death matter and requires a depth of emotion that is sometimes uncomfortable.

I cannot say God answers that prayer every day, it is not always necessary for me to beg someone to listen to the message of Jesus. Even though it has been many years since I first prayed that prayer, sometimes God does answer it. I remember one such occasion. We had been traveling and preaching in Germany for a month. The last couple of weeks had been spent doing a sports camp in conjunction with a church we had been assisting for a couple of years. At the camp, we had invited all the kids to a final special event. Wonderfully, close to 300 kids showed up at **Cross Point**, of which only about 30-40 of them came from the church's youth group. The youth pastor told me the rest were what they call *gangster kids* from the streets. Many of them were immigrants from Russia and other Eastern European countries. It is impossible to know exactly how many of them there were. They sat on the floor in the church sanctuary, packed wall-to-wall, out the back door, and even into the church courtyard.

The theme of the evening was ***Image is Nothing!*** There were some technical problems with the computers and lights, so we got a very late start. Then there was lots of music and a great skit from the youth drama team *Bobo and Friends.* They were an incredibly energetic and talented group—the proverbial *tough act to follow,* which is exactly what I had to do. It was after 10:00 PM as I got on the platform to preach and a large number of kids started getting up to leave. Remember, these were worldly kids directly from the streets, so politely sitting through *preaching* was not on their agenda.

I started preaching in German as fast as I could, desperately trying to regain their attention. I felt such an intense spiritual struggle in my heart. I knew this could easily be the first and only time many of these kids would truly hear the Gospel. I know that may sound overly dramatic, but in the context of secular Europe, that is no exaggeration. I desperately wanted them to hear about Jesus.

Not knowing what else to do, I suddenly dropped to my knees and begged them to listen to the most important thing they would ever hear. I didn't know how they would react to this, but I was wonderfully relieved to see it really worked. They sat back down. The room went completely silent and I sensed the Holy Spirit at work in their hearts. Their attention seemed riveted to the words of the Gospel. Still on my knees, I preached about being slaves to image and slaves to sin. I told them at length about the cross and that Jesus had purchased their freedom. I talked to them about Jesus standing at the door of their lives knocking, that they alone could open that door to Him. I was able to preach about twenty minutes in all. It was a glorious evening and I stayed until after midnight talking to individual kids about faith in Jesus.

On other occasions I have preached from my knees in the free speech zones of college campuses here in America to similar results. It definitely gets their attention. I am fully persuaded we must suspend *business as usual* and be willing to do whatever it takes to capture the hearts and minds of the generation of young people now on the brink of total spiritual ruin. We must see this situation for what it is, an emergency, and blow the trumpet. Like the Apostle Paul, we must warn them night and day with tears. They are worth it, and we must do all that is necessary to change their direction. Once we care and care deeply, we are ready to unleash one of the mightiest weapons of all against the forces holding this generation captive—prayer!

Chapter 14

Rediscovering the Power of Prayer

The diligent prayer life of mothers of the last generation for their wayward children is almost legendary! I have personally heard the testimony of many prodigals living in deplorable sin and rebellion against God. But even though sin did abound, God's grace did much more abound, because of a mother who burned the midnight oil in intercession before God for her lost child. They realized they were locked in a life and death struggle with the powers of darkness, crying out to God for mercy and salvation for their lost sheep.

As I speak to young people today, I sense they desperately need just that kind of prayer. Most of them are completely careless about their own spiritual condition, oblivious to the consequences of being lost eternally. We must care in their place! That is what intercessory prayer is all about. I truly believe the very soul of a generation hangs in the balance. We need to rediscover that mighty weapon of prayer; it is the greatest hope our kids have. If the lost condition of our children doesn't inspire mothers and fathers to intercessory prayer, I don't know what will.

As Paul said the mighty weapons of our warfare have the ability to demolish strongholds. Our fervent and simple prayers can destroy the very strongholds where this generation has been held captive. I realize as I begin this subject that it could certainly fill an entire book on its own. This volume is not intended as an exhaustive study of all types of prayer, so I will simply write about the specific kind of prayer that I believe it will take to awaken this generation—intercession. I will also try to encourage you by including my own testimony to the power of prayer.

I previously mentioned the enormous respect I now have for my grandmother's faith, so I will begin with a remarkable story of her prayer life. My grandmother died in 1978, and by the time of her death I was in no way demonstrating any desire to live for God. In fact, I was living a self-centered life in hot pursuit of all sin. I shudder now when I remember certain foolish episodes where my lifestyle could have completely destroyed my life. Let me simply say they were serious enough to have landed me in juvenile detention, maimed for life, or worse yet, dead and in hell.

Ultimately, I thank God for His mercy and grace. I believe much of that grace was obtained for me by the prayers of my godly grandmother. The book of Hebrews shows us that this is one of the chief functions of prayer. *Let us then approach the throne of grace with confidence, so that we may receive mercy and find grace to help us in our time of need (Hebrews 4:16 Emphasis added).* If ever there was a generation in desperate need of God's grace, this is it. We obtain that mercy and grace through prayer!

Nearly a year and a half after my grandmother died, I finally bowed my knee to the Lordship of Jesus and got saved. Several years after that, I encountered a sweet older lady named Minnie who gave me a clue about the kind of prayer life my Pentecostal grandmother must have had and how much she must have prayed for me. One afternoon, a friend and I were witnessing door to door in our town. We knocked on the door of an apartment and an older lady answered and invited us in. Through the conversation she not only told us she was already a believer, she also began to put things together and recognized me. As it turns out, she had been a very close friend of my grandmother. She knew of my mother and our family, and more specifically she knew of me.

During the conversation she called me by the name that only my family called me when I was growing up, and told me an amazing story. "Oh yes, your grandmother Mae prayed and prayed for you. She always called you her *preacher boy*, because God had told her you would be a preacher someday." I stopped her and said, "But grandma died in the summer of 1978, and I wasn't even saved until November 6th 1979. I didn't know myself that God had called me to preach until at least a year after becoming a Christian."

I was astounded! Nevertheless the timetable meant nothing to Minnie. She assured me God had let my grandmother in on that little secret long before she ever died. This story may be difficult to believe for some, but I know it is true. How I thank God for a grandma who prayed diligently for me. I believe she paved the way for me to not only enter the Kingdom of the Lord Jesus, but also for the ministry I have had for more than twenty-five years. Her prayer life inspires my prayer life today!

Intercession 101 * Just How Does God's Will Get Done?

The Lord Jesus, in scriptures' model prayer, helps us understand to some degree how God accomplishes His purposes down here on earth. Jesus explicitly instructed us to pray a specific prayer, *Your will be done on earth as it is in heaven!* [1] Obviously, our prayer life makes a difference in

127

just what happens on earth where God's will is concerned. Otherwise there would have been absolutely no reason whatsoever for Jesus to have told us to pray like this. In fact, if our prayers have no part in the equation as to how events unfold on earth, there is no reason to pray at all.

The Apostle Paul within scripture referred to certain things as *mysteries*. These are things that we, from our earthly perspective, can never fully grasp. Nevertheless, they are things we must simply believe and employ by trusting in God. I must say for me one of those mysteries is prayer; there is much about it I do not understand. God is undeniably the Sovereign Monarch of this entire universe. Why He would choose to involve us weak people in His plan is beyond me. But, scripture reveals He does in fact involve us, and prayer is an area I find most intriguing. God has a plan of redemption for humans on this planet and part of bringing that plan to pass involves our prayers.

Paul especially mentions a brother in the book of Colossians who obviously made a difference with his prayers. *Epaphras, who is one of you and a servant of Christ Jesus, sends greetings. He is <u>always wrestling in prayer</u> for you, that you may stand firm in all the will of God, mature and fully assured (Colossians 4:12 Emphasis added).* The implication is too obvious to miss; if Epaphras had not been willing to wrestle in prayer, the Colossian church members would not have stood firm in all of God's will.

I don't think many modern Christians think of this subject in terms of *wrestling in prayer*, but that is exactly what this brother did. We must realize struggle is involved, but it is worth it. Over and over throughout scripture in both the Old and New Testaments, God's Word very expressly couples together the unfolding of events on earth to the prayers of His people. Our calling out to Him in prayer is directly related to His will being done on earth.

Our prayer life makes a world of difference in the lives of those for whom we pray. James, the half brother of our Lord Jesus, gave us one of the Bible's greatest encouragements in prayer. ***The prayer of a righteous man is powerful and effective (James 5:16b).***

God chooses to mix our prayers into the equation of His will taking place on earth. The way I look at it, I don't have to know the myriad of complex engineering information that allows a jet liner to fly, to board one and soar across the earth. Likewise, I don't have to understand why God has chosen to do things the way He has; I only know He has commanded us to pray, *Your will be done on earth.* I recently heard a minister at a prayer breakfast discussing this same mystery. He reduced it down to this: *If we don't, He won't.* We must not shrink back from a rich and powerful prayer life. The Prophet Samuel said, ***far be it from me that I should sin against the Lord by failing to pray for you.***[2]

It goes without saying this generation of young people desperately needs our prayers. Our intercession can make a monumental difference. I honestly had to ask myself if I truly believed that the downward spiral of so many in this generation could still be turned around. Prayer is based on faith, and according to Hebrews 11:1, faith is being sure of what we hope for. We must have a God-given hope to effectively begin to pray. I say *God-given* because I do not think we can manufacture such hope by mere human effort.

However, the Bible declares that our God is the God of all hope, and I can truly say I believe this generation cannot only be turned around but actually become the catalyst for one of the greatest global revivals we have ever seen (more about that later). However, we cannot deny the reality of the dismal trends now dragging millions upon millions of young people toward destruction. Much work will have to be done before any turn around can happen. The majority of that work will be done by God's people in intercessory prayer.

That is why **ALL** of us must learn the principles of this kind of prayer and go to work.

When people, through sin and rebellion, wind up on the wrong side of God, then God is perfectly justified to judge them. In fact, unless mercy is obtained, it is the inevitable consequence of sin. Some in modern Christendom may be tempted to believe it is not possible to actually get on the wrong side of a loving God. Those who believe that urgently need to re-read the Bible, and not filter out the hundreds of references to that very side of God's holy nature. People who do not acknowledge this reality will never be intercessors, because they believe nothing is at stake. Therefore they would never have the kind of motivation that it takes to wrestle in prayer.

However, the intercessor knows God's nature! Even though God is capable of judgment, He is slow to anger and quick to forgive, and **IF** we pray He will send mercy instead. In fact the intercessor knows God is just waiting, even seeking someone who will prevail upon His mercy. Sadly, in some generations, no one responds to God's call to pray.

"I looked for a man among them who would build up the wall and stand before me in the gap on behalf of the land so I would not have to destroy it, but I found none. So I will pour out my wrath on them and consume them with my fiery anger, bringing down on their own heads all they have done," declares the Sovereign Lord. Ezekiel 22:30-31

Chapter 15

Heroes of Prayer

Thankfully, God does find people who understand this vital calling of prayer and respond. Dietrich Bonhoeffer, the German theologian who ultimately laid down his life for the faith in Hitler's Germany, once said, "To make intercession means to grant our brother the same right that we have received, mainly to stand before Christ and share in His mercy. This makes it clear, that intercession is also a daily service we owe to God and our brother. He who denies his neighbor the service of praying for him, denies him the service of a Christian."

Some of the greatest examples of this kind of prayer come to us from the pages of the Old Testament. Many, many times the faithful prayer ministry of Moses was the only thing that stood between the children of Israel and destruction. The most well-known example of these, the fiasco with the golden calf, gives us valuable insight into the heartfelt cry of the intercessor.

Then the Lord said to Moses, "Go down, because your people, whom you brought up out of Egypt, have become corrupt. They have been quick to turn away from what I commanded them and have made themselves an idol cast in the shape of a calf. They have bowed down to it and sacrificed to it and have said, 'These are your gods, O Israel, who brought you up out of Egypt.'

"I have seen these people," the Lord said to Moses, "and they are a stiff-necked people. Now leave me alone so that my anger may burn against them and that I may destroy them. Then I will make you into a great nation."

But Moses sought the favor of the Lord his God, "O Lord," he said, "why should your anger burn against your people, whom you brought out of Egypt with great power and a mighty hand? Why should the Egyptians say, 'It was with evil intent that he brought them out, to kill them in the mountains and to wipe them off the face of the earth?' Turn from your fierce anger; relent and do not bring disaster on your people. Remember your servants Abraham, Isaac and Israel, to whom you swore by your own self: 'I will make your descendants as numerous as the stars in the sky and I will give your descendants all this land I promised them, and it will be their inheritance forever.'" Then the Lord relented and did not bring on his people the disaster he had threatened (Exodus 32:7-14).

Perhaps the most detailed account of this *earthly-heavenly interaction* is Abraham's gallant attempt in prayer to stave off the destruction of Sodom and Gomorrah found in Genesis, chapter eighteen. God was basically fed up with the extreme perversity and wickedness saturating these two cities, and determined to amputate this infectious limb before it spread to the whole region. But amazingly before He did,

He wanted to discuss the matter with His earthly friend. *Then the Lord said, "Shall I hide from Abraham what I am about to do?" (Genesis 18:17).* What a glorious example of just how much God wants us involved in His plans, and the level of intimacy He extends to us as mere humans. In verses 20-21 God laid out His grievous case and the charges He was bringing against the inhabitants of these cities.

Abraham remained standing before the Lord and approached Him. He knew God's nature intimately. He also knew there were at least some righteous people in those cities, including some of his own family members—his nephew Lot and his family. So he began to plead with God in prayer: *Will you sweep away the righteous with the wicked? What if there are fifty righteous people in the city? Will you really sweep it away and not spare the place for the sake of the fifty righteous people in it? Far be it from you to do such a thing—to kill the righteous with the wicked, treating the righteous and the wicked alike. Far be it from you! Will not the Judge of all the earth do right? (Genesis 18:23b-25).* Notice the tone of Abraham's prayer, bold but not irreverent or disrespectful. I believe this kind of conversation could have only taken place in the context of two parties who were intimately acquainted with one another. They were both familiar with one another's character, they understood each other.

God wonderfully responded to Abraham's plea: *The Lord said, "If I find fifty righteous people in the city of Sodom, I will spare the whole place for their sake" (Genesis 18:26).* There nestled in this tedious negotiating session between God and Abraham we find the beautiful gem of all intercession! God is more than willing to spare multitudes of wicked people for the sake of the righteous. Our prayer on their behalf is enough to stave off the judgment they so richly deserve.

Even though the sinner does not truly deserve God's mercy, nevertheless, it can be obtained for him by the prayer of the righteous. God was willing to spare the **whole place** for the sake of the righteous. This principle fuels the hope and confidence of all those who cry out to God on behalf of others and it is our great hope for this generation as well.

Abraham continued his sacred plea bargaining with the Judge of the universe, again with a mix of boldness and genuine humility: ***Then Abraham spoke up again: "Now that I have been so bold as to speak to the Lord, though I am nothing but dust and ashes, what if the number of the righteous is five less than fifty? Will you destroy the whole city because of five people?" "If I find forty-five there," he said, "I will not destroy it" (Genesis 18:27-28).***

Seeing God's willingness to negotiate, so to speak, emboldened Abraham, and he began to probe the limits of God's mercy. Back and forth they wrestled with how many righteous people God would require to completely spare the cities. God responded each time with mercy. Finally, Abraham reached an agreement with God that if even ten could be found He would spare the whole place for their sake. Abraham must have simply assumed that was enough, surely ten righteous people could be found in these cities. Would God have gone even lower? We will perhaps never know, because at that point Abraham ceased his prayer on behalf of the residents of Sodom and Gomorrah.

Sadly, not even ten godly people could be found in this debacherous place and God sent fire and brimstone down on these wicked cities. However, due to the prayer of His faithful friend Abraham, God went to incredible lengths to remove his family before unleashing His fury. He sent two angels to evacuate Lot and his entire family, even going so far as to literally take them by the hand and lead them safely out of the city.[1]

Another example that is just too rich to pass by is that of Daniel. He also gives us a fascinating look right into the very heart of a true hero of prayer. He, along with the rest of his people, was experiencing firsthand the horrible consequence of national disobedience to God. This godly young Jewish man, a mere teenager, watched Jerusalem conquered by the ruthless Babylonian empire. He, along with some of his closest friends, was carried off as a slave to serve King Nebuchadnezzar in the city of Babylon. But this extraordinary young man did not become bitter or ungodly. On the contrary, he walked faithfully with God through enormous upheaval and pressure to conform to idolatrous customs, of not only the Babylonian, but later the Medo-Persian empire. He grew to be a great prophet and agent for change by his uncompromising commitment to a fervent life of prayer.

One interaction with God found in the ninth chapter of Daniel gives us an up-close glimpse into the beautiful godly heart that beat inside of this devout man of God. First, we see despite the shifting political landscape and ever changing belief system of those around him, Daniel stayed anchored to the eternal Word of God. His reference point remained the scriptures, and this gave him understanding and insight into exactly what was happening spiritually in the situation where he lived. *In the first year of Darius son of Xerxes (a Mede by descent), who was made ruler over the Babylonian kingdom—in the first year of his reign, I, Daniel, understood from the Scriptures, according to the word of the Lord given to Jeremiah the prophet, that the desolation of Jerusalem would last seventy years (Daniel 9:1-2).*

We too live in a time when moral values and spiritual knowledge has been turned on its head. We must stick unswervingly to the scripture to maintain God's true perspective. Daniel's knowledge of the Word of God inspired and motivated him in prayer. *So I turned to the Lord God and pleaded with him in prayer and petition, in fasting, and in sackcloth and ashes (Daniel 9:3).* Like Abraham many years before when ungodliness prevailed in the land, Daniel pleaded with God on behalf of the people. I love that specific verbiage, *pleaded with him.* It captures some of the fervency and depth of emotion with which he approached God.

He did not just send up some momentary sentimental generic *God bless everyone* prayer, instead he made a radical commitment to seek God in a serious manner. He pleaded, he fasted, and he put on the garments of repentance and extreme humility—sackcloth and ashes. He set aside business as usual and consecrated himself to God to find an answer for the lost generation around him.

> *I prayed to the Lord my God and confessed: "O Lord, the great and awesome God, who keeps his covenant of love with all who love him and obey his commands, we have sinned and done wrong. We have been wicked and have rebelled; we have turned away from your commands and laws. We have not listened to your servants the prophets, who spoke in your name to our kings, our princes and our fathers, and to all the people of the land. Lord, you are righteous, but this day we are covered with shame—the men of Judah and people of Jerusalem and all Israel, both near and far, in all the countries where you have scattered us because of our unfaithfulness to you" (Daniel 9:4-7).*

We have so much to learn from Daniel's prayer. First, even though all of scripture indicates Daniel himself was not guilty of any of these ungodly sins, as intercessor he put himself in the place of those he was praying for. He prayed in their stead. This is perhaps the second great key of intercessory prayer!

Secondly, he does not hurry past or sweep under the rug the precise sins of his generation. He stated unconditionally, even emphatically every possible way they had offended God. He very specifically nails down the thing they were so guilty of—they had flatly ignored God's ways and His laws. He acknowledges the heartfelt shame of that sin before God. Practically, without taking a breath in verses eight through twelve, he continues listing the ways his generation had sinned against God and how richly they deserved the punishment they were receiving. But, in verse nine, he drops the first hint of the hope of all hopes for the intercessor, *The Lord our God is merciful and forgiving, even though we have rebelled.*

Despite the grievous sin of the people, he still believed God was even richer in mercy and could forgive. Today, we seem to feel conflict and tension with these two dynamics, the guilt of people and the goodness of God to forgive. Unlike Daniel, we tend to minimize the guilt of people. More often we convey the idea that *God will forgive you because you're really not a bad person.* But in prayer, where all pretense melts before the fiery holiness of God, such anemic ideas are quickly obliterated. In verse thirteen he again acknowledges the need for repentance: *Just as it is written in the Law of Moses, all this disaster has come upon us, yet we have not sought the favor of the Lord our God by turning from our sins and giving attention to your truth.*

In verses fourteen through sixteen he continues unabated, on and on to confess the guilt and sin of the people of Israel. The bulk of his prayer is an acknowledgment before God of the wrongs of his generation. He does not, as our generation seems to do, diminish the importance of this concept. He sees it for what it is, the impediment blocking revival and the blessing of God. Not until verse nineteen does he finally actually beseech God for pardon: *O Lord, listen! O Lord, forgive! O Lord, hear and act! For your sake, O my God,*

do not delay, because your city and your people bear your Name.

Interestingly, of his prayer that covers fifteen verses, the first fourteen deal almost exclusively with guilt and sin, leaving only one verse actually asking for forgiveness. God apparently was delighted with this ratio, for He dispatched none other than the angel Gabriel himself to personally bring Daniel the message that his prayer had been heard on high and the answer had been granted! In fact, Daniel prayed this way for twenty one days straight before his angelic visit.[2]

If this generation of kids is going to receive the mercy and forgiveness of God, we like Daniel of old, are going to have to approach God with such humility, fervor, and the same pleasing *ratio* that delighted God. We too must learn the lessons provided by the heroes of prayer.

We must see the rampant sin running almost unchecked in our nation and even in our own Christian circles as the impediment to revival and blessing. We must not shy away from the uncomfortable confessing of sin and guilt; we must learn the art of balancing boldness and humility as we pray before a Holy God. We must tap into the same kind of prayer that gave these Old Testament heroes power with God to find mercy for the multitudes of their day.

O great and awesome God of Moses, Abraham, and Daniel, hear me in this generation. We have sinned and done wrong. We have been wicked and have rebelled; we have tuned away from your commands and laws. We have not sought the favor of the Lord our God by turning from our sins and giving attention to your truth.

We have not listened to your Holy Word. We have been unfaithful and we truly are covered in shame. Please forgive us for blasphemy and idolatry. We confess sexual immorality, promis-

cuity, and immodest dress has captured our land. Homosexuality and perversion flood our culture and threaten the very foundations of our society. We have loved worldliness and ungodly entertainment more than You, and have given too much of our time to such worthless things.

We have lost sight of Your holiness and need repentance and revival. Open our eyes and let us see a clear vision of You once again. Heal our land. Please withhold judgment from our youth and grant them repentance. Do not hold our sins and their sins against them, merciful God of heaven.

O Lord, listen! O Lord, forgive! O Lord, hear and act! For Your sake, O my God, do not delay, for we are in desperate need!

Chapter 16

Prayer That Won't Let Go!

A s we just learned, Daniel prayed for twenty-one days. That takes serious motivation and commitment. My grandmother prayed for years and died never seeing the answer to those prayers, but she obviously did not quit. In the New Testament Jesus taught about prayer that won't let go!

And He said to them, "Which of you shall have a friend, and go to him at midnight and say to him, 'Friend, lend me three loaves; for a friend of mine has come to me on his journey, and I have nothing to set before him;' and he will answer from within and say, 'Do not trouble me; the door is now shut, and my children are with me in bed; I cannot rise and give to you?' I say to you, though he will not rise and give to him because he is his friend, yet because of his <u>persistence</u> he will rise and give him as many as he needs.

"So I say to you, ask, and it will be given to you; seek, and you will find; knock , and it will be opened to you. For everyone who asks receives, and

he who seeks finds, and to him who knocks it will be opened" (Luke 11:5-10 NKJV Emphasis added).

Here from the mouth of Jesus, we learn that persistence is pleasing to God when it comes to our prayer life. Obviously, the man kept knocking until his friend got up and gave him the loaves of bread. From these words of Jesus we also learn another valuable thing about prayer—to ask, seek and knock. It is as if Jesus is letting us know that intensifying our effort in prayer is also not out of bounds—asking almost seems polite, seeking is a bit bolder, and knocking is designed to definitely get someone's attention.

I cannot help but notice that reversing this principle of *everyone who asks receives and he who seeks finds, and to him who knocks it will be opened*, makes a lot of sense as well. He who does not ask, does not receive, he who does not seek does not find, and if you do not knock, the door will never be opened for you. I am by nature a timid person, but because of these words of Jesus, I have learned that in prayer God is pleased when we are bold, not when we are bashful. James, the half brother of Jesus, boils it down to the simple concept: **"You do not have because you do not ask."** [1] But he adds a qualifier that filters out greedy or self-indulgent prayers.

Thankfully, when it comes to the subject at hand, asking, seeking, and knocking for the salvation and spiritual welfare of the young people all around us, selfishness is of no concern. We should boldly and persistently apply the principles that Jesus lays out here to interceding on behalf of this generation. Only a few chapters later, Jesus gives us another crystal clear example of this same principle. I believe He specifically did this because He knows how easy it is for us to lose heart and give up when we do not see the answers to our prayers.

Then Jesus told his disciples a parable to show them that they should always pray and not give up. He said: "In a certain town there was a judge who neither feared God nor cared about men. And there was a widow in that town who kept coming to him with the plea, 'Grant me justice against my adversary.'

"For some time he refused. But finally he said to himself, 'Even though I don't fear God or care about men, yet because this widow keeps bothering me, I will see that she gets justice, so that she won't eventually wear me out with her coming!'"

And the Lord said, "Listen to what the unjust judge says. And will not God bring about justice for his chosen ones, who cry out to him day and night? Will he keep putting them off? I tell you, he will see that they get justice, and quickly. However, when the Son of Man comes, will he find faith on the earth?" (Luke 18:1-8).

Jesus' words in this passage are saturated with God's wisdom. First of all, He says we should always pray and not give up! The opposite of giving up is to keep on praying. We dare not give up on our kids and their eternal well-being, so even when we don't know what else to do, we should keep on praying for them.

The parable itself reinforces the concept of persistence in prayer. It says, *for some time the judge refused,* but apparently this woman would not give up. The judge states his only motive for granting her justice is so *she won't eventually wear me out with her coming!* At first it seemed strange to me, this idea of wearing God out with a request in prayer. Growing up, we called that *harping on something* and it was a big **no, no.** Here Jesus encourages us to do that very thing, and lets us know beyond any shadow of doubt that God likes it.

A beautiful example of this can be found in the Book of Isaiah. *For Zion's sake I will not keep silent, for Jerusalem's sake I will not remain quiet, till her righteousness shines out like the dawn, her salvation like a blazing torch (Isaiah 62:1).* Here on display, we see the prophet's great love, affection, and concern for the beloved people of Jerusalem. In prayer, he pledges to not keep silent until her righteousness and salvation shine like a blazing torch. He does not just pledge **himself** to that kind of prayer, he recruits others for this kind of intercession: *You who call on the Lord, give yourselves no rest, and give him no rest till he establishes Jerusalem and makes her the praise of the earth (Isaiah 62:6b-7).*

Oh how practically and wonderfully this translates into our situation. Certainly we love our young people as much as Isaiah loved the inhabitants of Jerusalem. We should not keep silent until the righteousness and salvation found only in Christ is on display in their lives like a blazing torch. God Himself, through His Word, has specifically asked us not to rest or give Him any rest until He establishes them in righteousness! Ask God to give you the grace and motivation to have that kind of prayer life for young people. I think sometimes we bog down trying to find *magic words* when we pray and intercede, or we grope around in the dark not knowing what to pray at all, but Jesus made it so simple. The ones who get answers from the Father are the ones *who cry out to him day and night.*

He promises if we will simply be faithful to cry out to Him day and night that we will get justice or the answers to the things we are praying about. Then Jesus really seals the whole idea of His expectations of us—persistence in prayer. He closes the passage with the slightly frightening question, *However, when the Son of Man comes, will he find faith on the earth?* He seems to be making it quite clear that this is what He wants to find us doing, calling out to Him day and night in persistent prayer when He returns. When my Master comes back I don't want to be found lazing away, enjoying the good things in life, I want to be about His business. Obviously, laboring in prayer is something He expects. As long as I perceive spiritual danger looming on the horizon for this generation of young people, I want to be calling out to God night and day for their salvation and spiritual well-being.

Praying for Twenty-five Years!

I wish I had more testimonies from my own life about hanging in there in persistent prayer until the answer comes. I do have one I would like to share as a means of encouragement to you. When I got saved in 1979, I immediately began to seriously grasp the implications of a person losing their soul. At that time, I had no evidence that my dad had ever made a profession of faith in his entire life. I felt sure he was not right with God.

This troubled me deeply as a young believer, so as a baby Christian I began to pray for his salvation. Being young in faith, I did not have a clue about the subject of intercession, but with child-like faith I did the best I could. Years passed and things did not improve. I would become discouraged and would lapse into being less than diligent in those prayers. Then I would feel convicted and renew my efforts in prayer.

I invited him to church and there were occasional events, Easter plays and concerts, where he would actually come. I would seize any opportunity to tell him about faith in Christ. Later, as I moved into ministry, he would come to services where I was preaching, but none of it ever brought a profession of faith.

Decades went by and I went to the mission field. He seemed proud of that, but still no evidence that he was ready to repent of his sins and bow his knee to Christ. Other family members made professions, but not my dad. Sometimes I would pray diligently every day for weeks or even months. He was always at the top of my prayer list. I had not yet learned the things I have shared in this book about persistence in prayer and I admit months would go by when I did not pray.

There were so many times when it would look like things were worse than ever. Then God's Spirit would stir my heart and I would start praying diligently. My dad began to get older, into his sixties, and then seventies, still no discernable movement toward God. I was so aware that, at least statistically, almost no one becomes a Christian at his age. The thought of my dad dying without Christ and spending eternity in hell tormented me. It never ceased to be a motivating factor for me; I would ramp up the intensity of crying out to God for his salvation. I would pray, *Lord, your arm is not too short to save. You are faithful to your promises. Please don't hold his sins against him on Judgment Day. Forgive him; draw him by the power and conviction of your Holy Spirit. Let him bow his knee to Jesus.* Sometimes I would simply pray: *Lord I don't know how you're going to do it, but I'm asking you to save his soul.*

By 2005, I was praying harder than ever but battling the demons of doubt more than ever. I knew plenty of people died at his age, and he still wasn't saved. Then for the first time in his life his health failed and he got very sick. After weeks in the hospital, one day he called me into his room and made everyone else leave. He wanted to talk about his life and spiritual things. We had three beautiful sweet hours to talk about the issues at hand. Mercifully, he got better and left the hospital.

After praying for more than twenty-five years, when my dad had regained his strength, he made a profession of faith! I had the privilege of baptizing him, along with my sister and her husband. Now he reads the Bible and attends church, and has had a season of good health.

I have wept at different times before the Lord, thanking Him for His faithfulness to do what seemed at times like the impossible. He hears our prayers! I look forward to spending eternity with my dad in heaven with Jesus!!! I have to admit, I did his baptism a little differently than the dozens of others I have had the privilege of conducting. Normally, once I get the person's face below the surface, I immediately bring them back up. But in dad's case, the moment was so sweet for me, I held him under just a second or two longer. I wanted to savor the faithfulness and mercy of God!

I encourage you today in prayer, **NEVER GIVE UP!** If you are praying for people to be saved, keep on praying. Cry out to God day and night, He is faithful to hear and answer our prayers. I also encourage you if you have children or grandchildren who are not walking with the Lord, or simply want to serve God in intercession and prayer, begin to pray for young people all around you by name. Pray for all the kids in your youth group at church, or for the kids in your city. People at our church are now praying over pictures of the young people in our schools' yearbooks.

Don't stop there. Paul encourages us with this amazing exhortation: *I urge, then, first of all, that requests, prayers, intercession and thanksgiving be made for everyone (1 Timothy 2:1).* This admonition is truly awesome! The Living Bible says it this way: *Here are my directions: Pray much for others; plead for God's mercy upon them; give thanks for all he is going to do for them.* I would encourage you to **pray for this entire generation!**

Jesus Rescues a Young Person From Darkness

One time Jesus encountered a distressed man whose child urgently needed to be rescued from spiritual bondage. *The next day, when they came down from the mountain, a large crowd met him. A man in the crowd called out, "Teacher, I beg you to look at my son, for he is my only child. A spirit seizes him and he suddenly screams; it throws him into convulsions so that he foams at the mouth. It scarcely ever leaves him and is destroying him. I begged your disciples to drive it out, but they could not" (Luke 9:37-40).*

The generation of young people now living on planet earth, like this boy, are being destroyed by the kingdom of darkness. They are on the brink of complete spiritual ruin, and they too need the ministry of Jesus to set them free. In Mark's Gospel, Jesus asks the man, *"How long has he been like this?" "From childhood," he answered (Mark 9:21b).* If we think the young are somehow off-limits or exempt from harm by the prince of evil and his dark forces in the arena of spiritual conflict, we are sadly mistaken.

Like ruthless terrorists target children, I believe our young people are especially singled out as targets by Satan. The dismal statistics and trends I have cited in this book are no secret. Practically no one doing youth ministry today could be unaware of the crisis situation we are in now. In fact, conferences, symposiums, and think tanks are gathering to address the issues now facing the church. We are losing almost an entire generation out the back door of the church at graduation. However, thus far nothing has made a dent in changing the direction of America's lost youth. I'm happy that at least now the problem is being acknowledged by some and people are seeking answers to this alarming trend.

But, if we do not possess the spiritual power and knowledge to set them free, we are just like Jesus' early disciples. The man had already sought their anemic help, and was forced to exclaim, *I begged your disciples to drive it out, but they could not.* Of course this man's story had a happy ending. After a very brief spiritual clash, Jesus drove out the evil spirit, healed the boy, and gave him back to his father.[2]

Our situation is less sure. We are talking about millions upon millions of young people with no sense of spiritual direction or value, and like the young man in the story, their lives are being destroyed.

We too should have the same humble attitude of Jesus' followers that day. *After Jesus had gone indoors, his disciples asked him privately, "Why couldn't we drive it out?" (Mark 9:28).* We too must come to grips with our failure to capture the hearts of the children who have been raised in church. We must grasp the gravity of the consequences of not turning this generation around. We must seek Jesus' counsel and help with great humility. I believe His answer to those first disciples should also speak to our heart today: *So He said to them, "This kind can come out by nothing but prayer and fasting" (Mark 9:29 NKJV).*

We must apply these words of Jesus with all haste. We desperately need <u>MORE PRAYER</u> and fasting on behalf of young people all around us who are captive to sin and destructive behavior. Not only do we need to pray, we need to apply the maximum amount of spiritual force possible to obtaining their salvation. That should include one of God's great tools for doing so—fasting. The thought of close to 95% of our church kids throwing away the faith at graduation should alarm us. The thought of untold millions more young people in our culture who have **never** been exposed to the message of Jesus at all, should alarm us. They are running down the broad road that leads to destruction full speed ahead. If this situation does not merit fasting then nothing does.

Daniel did not just pray when he desired to obtain God's mercy for his generation, he also fasted. In modern times we have a saying, *If you keep doing the same thing, you will keep getting the same results.* I believe any time we come up against spiritual strongholds, things that just will not seem to move, we can up-the-ante, as it were, by fasting. Fasting provides breakthroughs that will come no other way. We need to skip some meals, television, and other activities. We need to devote that time to God, where we can lift up in prayer the generation of youth who so desperately need to experience a life changing touch from God's Spirit.

The Bible says that when Noah was ***warned about things not yet seen, in holy fear built an ark to save his family.***[3] We too must build an ark of safety in our day and age for our loved ones, especially our kids. We must use the same tools Noah did, faith and trust in God! Prayer is ultimately an exercise of faith and trust. God responds to it and we engage God by crying out to Him night and day—by persisting, by not letting go of His promises. Prayer has always been utilized in God's Kingdom to bring about change, to obtain mercy and grace in a time of need. This generation so desperately needs just such a change. Let us respond to God's time-honored method for the healing of His people.

If my people, who are called by my name, will humble themselves and pray and seek my face and turn from their wicked ways, then will I hear from heaven and will forgive their sin and will heal their land. 2 Chronicles 7:14

O God, bring back the prodigals in this generation; let them come to themselves and cry out, "Father, I have sinned against You and heaven!" Your arm is not too short to save, and we ask that You would stretch it out in the name of Your holy Son Jesus to miraculously save a generation from destruction. Lead them not into temptation, and deliver them from evil. They are sheep without a shepherd, harassed and helpless and we plead with You to send out workers into the harvest field of young people in this nation who are so unacquainted with Your ways.

And Lord, open their hearts and minds to respond to Your message. Let Your Word spread rapidly through this generation; let it be honored. Give them ears to hear what Your Spirit has to say. We pray for revival and awakening among our youth. Make them acutely aware of You. Let them hunger and thirst after righteousness. Let Christ be formed in them!

Bottom line, we cry out to You day and night for their salvation. We leave the details to You. Spare Your people O Lord. Let them be right with You on Judgment Day. Let the blood of Jesus cleanse them from all sin. Let them walk with You in paradise for eternity. You are gracious, slow to anger and abounding in love. We are convinced that You are able to guard what we have entrusted to You against that day!

Chapter 17

Saved at Last!

I have shared my confusing experiences at two very different churches as a young teen, as well as the prayer life of my godly Pentecostal grandmother. But I have not yet said how I finally came to real and lasting faith in Jesus Christ. After my *church experiences*, I not only continued in my pursuit of sin, I plunged deeper than ever into self-indulgence and immorality. I shudder to put into print all that I was then. I smashed God's commandments daily without remorse. I lied every single day to get by and hide the bad stuff I was doing. Like most teenage boys, I followed my hormones and lived by the philosophy of my day, *if it feels good, do it!* My language was not only raunchy and laced with filthy words, it was full of blasphemy. As a southern boy I was also a racist and a rebel in almost every sense of the word. A popular song was about being on a highway to hell, and I surely was.

Other than the occasional thought of being spewed out of Jesus' mouth, I didn't think much about God. On November 6th 1979, when I was seventeen years old, a pretty girl in one of my classes asked me if I wanted to have pizza with her that night. I thought she was talking about a date, so I ecstatically said, "I would love to do that!" "Great," she said, "we are having a pizza party at my church."

Oh no, I thought, *this chic has tricked me into going to church. I know what that is all about, stained glass, hard pews, and long sermons.* But the combination of a pretty girl, pizza, and being too embarrassed to renege when I had already said yes, kept me from backing out. She told me the name of the church, the time of the *service*, and where it was located. As it turned out, Crestmont Baptist Church was located only a couple of miles from my house on a street we traveled practically every day.

That evening, I drove to the church and walked in all by myself. That doesn't seem like a big deal, but I think it was the first time in my life I had walked into a church all alone. I moved rather quickly through the foyer and into the back door of the sanctuary. I felt uneasy and out of place. We had rarely gone to church growing up, so other than my two confusing experiences at churches as a teenager, it all seemed strange to me. It was a church of several hundred and I scanned to see the girl from my school and her family. Even though it was nearly time for the service to start, they were nowhere to be found. I felt so conspicuous there in the aisle, almost like I had a giant sign around my neck that said: I DON'T BELONG HERE! I scooted into the back pew, sat down, and tried to look invisible.

Thankfully, with only a minute to spare, my friend and her mom showed up. They, of course, headed for a pew closer to the front. I had seen them but they had not yet seen me, so I made a bee-line over to them. It was good to at least know one person in the building. I think we sang a couple of hymns and there were a couple of announcements. Then we all headed over to the fellowship hall. The pizza was home-made on huge flat cookie sheets. We sat in folding chairs and ate at folding tables. I don't remember much about our conversation, except that it was awkward at best. Then we all headed back to the sanctuary for the real service.

Of course I had no idea at the time, but I had inadvertently walked right into a full blown youth revival designed to do only one thing, save my eternal soul. After a few more hymns, a man stood up to preach. I don't remember much about him except they told me he was an *evangelist*. Not that I knew what that was. What I do remember was he was very direct and spoke with fiery conviction. I can't tell you everything he said other than it was very basic. He spoke about sin, the fact that I would someday face God on Judgment Day when I died, and that Jesus had died on the cross for my sins. When he spoke about the cross, this touched my heart in a way that is totally indescribable. I knew the nail holes in Jesus' hands and feet were there because of my sin.

It is difficult to explain. I can't say that this information was completely new to me, but this night there was something different about it. His words hit me with the force of a sledgehammer; they were accompanied with a very real and undeniable authority! It made sense on a very deep level, not just mentally. It seemed to reach the very core of my soul. I felt like the very God of the universe was speaking directly to me and that I was very much responsible for every wrong thing I had ever done.

The only way I can describe it was like getting in trouble at school. I knew intuitively I was guilty and was in trouble with a Holy God. It was odd, but I took it so personal that by the time he got to the end of his message, my heart was pounding in my chest and I knew something would be required of me. All this was going on internally. I knew my school friend and her mom were completely oblivious to my inner turmoil. I was totally aware that something had to be done, but I had no idea what.

That soon became perfectly clear. The evangelist instructed us to bow our heads and close our eyes. Then he gave the *invitation.* If we wanted to accept Christ he instructed us to come to the front. Now my heart was really pounding. I felt like I should go, but that would blow my cover. I was sure my friend was still unaware of what was going on inside of me. This tug of war went on for several minutes. I couldn't imagine squeezing past everybody on that crowded pew and stepping into the aisle. Finally, he closed the service—maybe I was off the hook.

My friend and her mom made some small talk and said they were glad I had come. I slipped quietly out the back door. Once outside, I quickened my pace and disappeared into my yellow Ford Pinto. I felt if I could get away from this church and these people all these feelings would go away. I was wrong; God's Spirit was still there! Even when I arrived home and was all alone in my room, I felt just as compelled that I had to respond to Jesus' message. Finally, I could stand it no longer; I got on my knees beside my bed and a prayer instinctively came from the depths of my heart. I asked Jesus to forgive my sins. I wanted the pardon that He paid for on the cross, and I wanted to follow Him. I prayed that He would now become my Lord and master!

I not only got saved that night, I prayed similar prayers every night for several weeks. I wanted to be absolutely sure, so on my knees in the presence of Jesus, I began working out my salvation with fear and trembling. You might think that is bad theology, but personally I'm glad it happened that way. I feared God and I wanted to be completely certain I was really saved!

In a great many ways my life instantly changed. I repented and turned from things I knew to be sin. I no longer blasphemed God or cursed. I no longer pursued girls for my own gratification. All I wanted from the moment I got saved was to have a godly wife with whom to serve Jesus. I repented of and completely changed my racist views; after all, who was I to think I was superior to anyone for whom Jesus had bled and died? In fact, I had what seemed like a river of love coming out of my heart for everyone of every color. I knew it was from God because I had never felt this kind of love for people before I was saved.

I started going to that same church every Sunday. Now those people, who seemed so strange to me that first night, were truly my brothers and sisters. I loved them so much I felt like I would have died for them if necessary. Best of all, little by little, I started discovering the Bible and read it often. Encountering the beautiful promises from God for the first time was better than finding rubies and diamonds.

My attitude about my parents changed. I was still an immature teenager who didn't want to clean my room or take out the trash, but I made a conscious effort to obey and honor my parents. Other habits took longer to break. I still listened to rock music that glorified all the things I no longer believed in. Bit by bit that kind of music no longer expressed anything that was in my heart. I threw my beloved eight tracks into the trash and replaced them with contemporary Christian music. Now the music of Dallas Holm, The Imperials, The Cruise Family, and Keith Green resonated with what was going on in my heart.

When those fiery evangelists came (which they often did in my first ten years of going to church) and turned up the heat during the invitation and asked, *If you were to die tonight, are you sure you would go to heaven?* I had complete peace inside! I knew beyond any shadow of doubt that I was born again and would spend eternity with Jesus, my King. Oh, how I thank God for His mercy for me! I praise Him for sending His Son to die on the cross so I could receive a pardon! I thank Him for sending me His message through an obedient servant who was not ashamed of it. I have now had the privilege of walking with and serving Jesus for more than twenty-five years. The Bible says, *If anyone is in Christ, he is a new creation; the old has gone, the new has come! (2 Corinthians 5:17).* That is truly the story of my life.

It is not hard for me to figure out why I finally came to saving faith in the Lord Jesus. It is because I heard an evangelist who did not *beat around the bush*; who was not ashamed of the Gospel and declared it in a direct and straight-forward manner. He spoke of my sin and the reality that I would stand before God, completely guilty on Judgment Day. By the time he finished his message, I felt deeply convicted and knew I needed to get right with God. He declared the Gospel in just the way I needed to hear it—strong and direct. He also preached the Gospel in the way I almost **never** hear it proclaimed these days—strong and direct!

Chapter 18

Gospel *Lite*

I'm so glad I got saved in 1979. I doubt very seriously I would have ever been so radically changed by contemporary preaching. I don't think I would have responded at all to most of what I hear today proclaimed as *gospel*. What am I talking about? The Gospel doesn't change, right? The truth is the *gospel* has undergone a radical transformation since I first became a Christian. After hearing God's call, attending Bible College, living on the mission field, and serving in ministry for a decade, a definite change began to occur in the way the Gospel was presented.

About 1995, for the first time, I started becoming aware that much of the church was moving in a new direction. At first I was open to some of the changes; they seemed innocuous and even helpful. They primarily involved stylistic changes in the way worship services looked. Most of the congregation and even the ministers got rid of their fancy clothes and became more *casual*. I cannot say that I have missed wearing a tie and coat every time I go to church or preach. I know this is important to some people and that is fine. There is basically nothing right or wrong about *dressing up* for church. God's primary focus is on what is in our heart, not how fancy our clothes are. Other than the issues of modesty and pretentiousness, how we dress is not dealt with in the New Testament.

However, it was not just our dress that became laid-back; our entire approach to God and His Word started becoming more casual. About that time a great many churches began to adopt a new user-friendly *ministry philosophy.* I acknowledge there may have been some changes in style that needed to happen and I believe some truly good things also occurred during this same season. In fact, I'm not at all against stylistic changes when it comes to reaching people. No one could look at my ministry over the last quarter of a century and accuse me of not being able to *think outside the box.* However, I admit I steadfastly refuse to *think outside the Book!*

In our desire to *do church* or even outreach in an informal and relaxed way, we have lost something else that is very valuable. Much like the *side effects* of last decade's wonder drugs that show up later to haunt the pharmaceutical company, the church in America is in many ways experiencing side effects of new ministry philosophies. What has become perfectly clear is in our desire to become **laid-back,** we have in far too many cases instead become **lukewarm.** We know that is extremely displeasing to the Lord Jesus. The area where our casualness is most perceptible is in the message we deliver to the world.

The great catch-phrase that took root in regard to the message the church is now delivering to the world from the pulpit became **positive and uplifting!** So, in tune with that philosophy, the modern *gospel* advances the idea that Jesus came to rescue us from a meaningless life, not so much from sin and judgment. It is undeniable that a purposeful swing has been made away from references to the harsher realities of God's Word. It has been documented by evangelical historians, by the most reliable Christian research groups, and even secular television and print news. The nature of this change is perfectly apparent in a string of secular newspapers and magazines that documented their perception of the church's *new and improved* message:

> **"As with all clergymen [this pastor's] answer is God—but he slips Him in at the end, and even then doesn't get heavy. No ranting, no raving. No fire, no brimstone. He doesn't even use the H-word. Call it light Gospel. It has the same salvation as the Old Time Religion, but with a third less guilt."** [1]

> **"[The pastor] is preaching a very upbeat message... It's a Salvationist message, but the idea is not so much being saved from the fires of hell. Rather, it's being saved from meaninglessness and aimlessness in this life. It's more of a soft-sell."** [2]

> **"The sermons are relevant, upbeat, and best of all, short. You won't hear a lot of preaching about sin and damnation and hell fire. Preaching here doesn't sound like *preaching*. It is sophisticated, urbane, and friendly talk. It breaks all the stereotypes."** [3]

> **"By most accounts, it [Hell] has all but disappeared from the pulpit rhetoric of mainline Protestantism. And it has fared only marginally better among evangelicals."** [4]

Slipping God in at the end and *even then not getting too heavy* is definitely the *soft-sell*. Sadly, it seems we really are preaching a kind of Gospel *Lite* to this generation, and the side effects are now mounting. Oh, how grievous that we are abandoning the clear straightforward teaching of scripture for modern witty friendly talks that do not have the most precious thing of all, the anointing of the Holy Spirit.

Nowhere in the pages of the New Testament can we find the concept of a soft-sell! Jesus said, **"Go into all the world and preach the gospel."** [5] The early church obeyed Him with passion and zeal, so much so that all but one of the apostles died brutal premature deaths because of their preaching. They gave their very lives for the message. They declared it unashamedly, and no price was too high to pass it on.

The reason I'm going to heaven is because in 1979 I heard the Words of the Lord Jesus. The only reason I heard those words is because an evangelist that night preached from a Bible. The only reason he had a Bible is because Christians down through the ages paid an unimaginable price to pass that life-changing message along. We must never, never forget that our New Testament came to us through prison bars, from blood-stained hands. We must declare it and declare it all. I'm afraid John MacArthur, Jr hit the nail on the head when he wrote that this generation is **ashamed of the Gospel.**[6]

Don't be tempted to think that *ministry philosophies* or what ministers preach have nothing to do with you if you are not a preacher. The message you are hearing has an enormous impact on how you think, how you live your life as a Christian, and how you pass along the faith to your children or grandchildren. You may have never thought of yourself as a minister, but numerous passages clearly indicate that as New Testament believers we all have a ministry.[7] While it may be true that you will never stand in a pulpit, Paul said our lives are like a letter read by all men.[8] That could not be more true than for our children. They read *the letter* of our lives more closely than anyone, so it is paramount that you understand the issues involved in how we present the Gospel today.

During my first ten years as a Christian, we had revivals preached by men who were not trying to be witty, urbane, or popular; they preached about sin, repentance, the cross, Jesus' return, heaven, and hell. These are subjects I almost never hear anymore. How different than the Apostle Paul's experience. After more than three years of ministry to the Ephesian Church, he was able to testify to those precious believers as they saw him for the last time on earth: *You know that I have not hesitated to preach anything that would be helpful to you but have taught you publicly and from house to house. I have declared to both Jews and Greeks that they must turn to God in repentance and have faith in our Lord Jesus (Acts 20:20-21).*

He did not shrink back or hesitate to preach **repentance** and **faith** in Jesus Christ. He knew his time was short, but his conscience was clear. Only four verses later he told the church elders something truly remarkable: *And now I know that none of you to whom I have preached the Kingdom will ever see me again. I declare today that I have been faithful. If anyone suffers eternal death, it's not my fault, for I didn't shrink from declaring all that God wants you to know (Acts 20:25-27 NLT).* Or as more traditional Bible versions say, Paul *declared the whole counsel of God.* As I pointed out earlier from this text, we also know the exact demeanor and content of his preaching. *Remember that for three years I never stopped warning each of you night and day with tears (Acts 20:31b Emphasis added).*

The idea of **warning** sinners almost never comes into play today. I'm not talking about being mean-spirited, nor am I saying we should be obnoxious. I **am** talking about preaching with the courage of conviction and warning young people about the consequences of rejecting Christ. I once had the privilege of hearing a very wise older minister who had been faithful to preach the full counsel of God for decades. In his sermon he gave us young preachers a glorious piece of advice. When asked about how he was able to still preach *hell fire* messages to modern sophisticated listeners, he replied, "You can preach any truth from the Word of God if you have tears in your eyes." I believe that is just what Paul did in his generation; he preached with tears in his eyes. I believe every generation will respond to the true Christian message if it is preached with passion and absolute conviction.

Not only do we no longer declare it with tears, we don't declare some of it at all. We have completely dropped what we consider the harsher or embarrassing parts. The secular newspaper and magazine reporters wryly noted when listening to these modern ministers, *you won't hear a lot of preaching about sin, fire, or the H-word.* I remember once after preaching in a large modern church a few years ago, a woman came up to me weeping and told me she had been attending there for almost five years. She was touched and thanked me for my message and said she had never heard any of these things before.

What is noteworthy is I had not preached anything off the chart or unusual, but rather the simple Gospel—our lost condition, our guilt before God, our appointment with death and judgment, and then the glorious cross of Jesus! I'm convinced many churches today are so busy preaching a witty sophisticated *self help* message that they have lost the real message of the New Testament. They are trying so hard to come across as upbeat and positive that they must completely neglect the Bible's actual message. The notions of sin, repentance, a Day of Judgment, and the Cross are considered completely old fashioned.

Why don't we preach about these things anymore? Are we ashamed? Jesus spoke frequently about all of these subjects. Are we more spiritual or wiser than our Lord? Paul was able to say that he had been faithful and had not hesitated to preach anything that would be helpful. He said, *I didn't shrink back from declaring the full counsel of God.* He was confident no one would suffer eternal death because he held back in delivering all of God's message.

Can we be so sure today? Can we not see the irreparable harm we are doing to our young people by not declaring to them the whole Gospel? Paul gave young Timothy this advice: ***Watch your life and doctrine closely. Persevere in them, because if you do, you will save both yourself and your hearers (1 Timothy 4:16).*** We would do well today to contemplate his meaning. In our day and time, even with the seemingly good intention of attracting the lost, we have inadvertently removed what we perceive to be those things in the Gospel that seem like a negative. I believe in far too many circles we are preaching a *gospel* that does not save! What we are preaching has not captured the heart of this generation — that is why they are leaving the church in droves at the first opportunity after graduation.

Chapter 19

The Message That Never Loses its Relevance

Another popular notion these days is we must keep our message relevant. However, too many speakers misinterpret this concept and use the idea to promote a *gospel* of self-help. Most messages now focus on finding happiness and meaning for our temporal life on earth—how to have a good marriage, good finances, good health, and a good life now! Although this sounds *oh so* relevant, the truth is, it simply gets lost in the shuffle. If I really want self help, I can get that from anyone of half a dozen afternoon talk shows. While the Bible is definitely filled with practical wisdom on these subjects, it offers something more. It is the Book of books, the most widely read, most influential piece of literature of all times.

What separates it from the crowd of innumerable volumes collecting dust in libraries around the world? It speaks with credibility about eternal issues! It answers with authority the deepest issues of the human heart and mind: *Who am I? Why am I here? Is this all there is to life? Is there life after death?* These are universal questions that have gnawed at the human psyche since recorded history. It also deals with finality with one of the most troubling and enduring questions. A question that plagues modern man as much as ancient man: *Why is there evil in the world? And how can we overcome it, on a global level, and more importantly, on a personal level?* God sent His Son into the world to model and demonstrate PURE PERFECTION! He sacrificed His very life to save us from judgment and rob sin of its power over us. He offers FORGIVNESS to all and the promise of eternal life with Him!

Our message completely loses its relevance when we refuse to include these primary Biblical ingredients. When we are working so hard to stay positive and upbeat, we lose the ability to really deal with the deepest issue of sin and evil. One's personal guilt before God will never fit into the category of *upbeat*, so it is largely neglected in many messages today. Jesus said: ***When he (the Holy Spirit) comes, he will convict the world of guilt in regard to sin and righteousness and judgment (John 16:8).***

That IS the missing ingredient, conviction of the Holy Spirit. The word conviction means to be convinced! Very few in the generation of young people living now have ever been convinced by God's Spirit of the Gospel's realities — primarily that we need a Savior from our sin. Jesus gave no indication that the Holy Spirit would convict the world of their meaningless life; He did however promise He would deal with us in regard to the subjects of guilt of our sin, righteousness, and judgment.

The reason that is so relevant is because we as humans have been created in the very image of God, and He has put within every man a conscience. That word comes to us from the Latin and means **Con** - with, **science** - knowledge. We are <u>with</u> the <u>knowledge</u> of God and the knowledge of right and wrong. If we are so afraid of offending people that we don't deal with this primary issue, we then become paralyzed and truly irrelevant. The majority of the Christian communication I hear today – TV, radio, books, and sermons preached – never deals with the very issues of which Jesus said the Holy Spirit would convince the world. He promised to convict them of their guilt of sin, that right-standing with God can only be obtained through repentance and faith, and that without that pardon **we will face God's judgment.**

Mediocre Grace, How Sweet the Sound!

Picture for a moment a guy sitting on a warm tropical beach. He is surrounded by beautiful girls in bikinis, sipping a cool rum punch. As the refreshing ocean breeze caresses his tanned skin and the girls rub suntan oil on his bulging muscles, I walk up and say, "Leave this wretched beach and come with me to the air-conditioned hotel over there so I can tell you how to find meaning in your life." He would probably look at me and question my mental health. "**Meaning in life?** I'm doing pretty well just like I am. No thanks!" At the very least, I would have a tough time persuading him to leave the beach. I'm sure my message would seem irrelevant to him.

But what if I walked up to the very same guy and said, "I just saw a report that there is a tsunami out there—a massive seventy foot wall of water will crash upon this very beach in about seven minutes. Leave this beach and come with me to the tenth floor of that massive concrete hotel over there." My message would be the most relevant information he could ever hear at that moment. Not only would he happily leave the beach with me, he would be profoundly thankful to me for bringing him the *good news!* He would likely be my friend for life.

This may sound silly to some, but for multitudes of modern people, including millions of young people, that is exactly how they hear the Gospel presented to them. They are sitting on the pleasant sunny beach and are more or less incredulous, if not completely mystified, by our insistence that they need to come to Jesus to find true happiness.

We now strive to give a consumer-driven crowd what we think they want, practical, entertaining, and completely inoffensive messages. The modern *gospel* conveniently makes little mention of the tsunami of God's judgment that will crash upon everyone at the Great White Throne. Could anyone even pretend to argue that the Bible does not promise a horrific end for anyone not in the Ark of salvation provided by Jesus at the cross? And yet more and more evangelical churches are abandoning the Bible's clear instructions and falling into the exact trap Paul warned us about 2,000 years ago.

> *Preach the Word; be prepared in season and out of season; correct, rebuke and encourage—with great patience and careful instruction. <u>For the time will come when men will not put up with sound doctrine. Instead, to suit their own desires, they will gather around them a great number of teachers to say what their itching ears want to hear. They will turn their ears away from the truth and turn aside to myths.</u> But you, keep your head in all situations, endure hardship, do the work of an evangelist, discharge all the duties of your ministry (2 Timothy 4:2-5 Emphasis added).*

We have all no doubt heard the adage, *I've got good news and I've got bad news. Which do you want to hear first?* People almost always choose to hear the bad news first. However, in our case one does not make sense without the other. We need to realize the **good news** of the Gospel seems absolutely irrelevant to someone who is completely unconvinced of the **bad news**. The bad news being that his soul will be eternally lost apart from the salvation of Jesus.

This was all such a mystery to me twenty-five years ago, when I first starting talking to lost people outside the walls of the church about faith. It seemed no matter how passionately I told them that God loved them and wanted to save them, people were for the most part completely uninterested in the matter of their eternal soul. I rarely had their attention.

Then one day it finally made sense. I was telling them how to be saved and they did not believe they were lost.[1] The *gospel* many are presenting today is trying so hard to be positive and upbeat that it NEVER mentions people's guilt before God and His ultimate judgment for the sinner. The truth is instead of actually highlighting God's grace, it makes grace considerably less than amazing. Get the tune to *Amazing Grace* in your mind and then sing the modern *gospel*'s version.

> **<u>Mediocre</u> grace, how sweet the sound,**
> **that saved a <u>NICE</u> guy like me.**
> **I was <u>NEVER</u> really lost, but now I'm found.**
> **Was <u>NEVER</u> blind, but now I see.**
> **Through <u>NO</u> dangers toils and snares, I have already come.**
> **'Tis grace hath brought me safe thus far,**
> **And grace will lead me...**
> **...<u>to a fulfilling life?</u>**

If John Newton had written his famous song with the above lyrics, I dare say it would have never become what it is today, perhaps the single most recognizable song in America. But, more than 200 years after its original composition, it still is heard thousands of times a year by even the most secular people in our nation. Not only do these new lyrics make its message completely senseless in nature, the song loses all its impact.

171

That is exactly the message the modern *gospel* presents. The secular mindset of today is, *Well, I would have probably made it to heaven regardless, because I'm a really good person anyway, but I guess it will be nice of God to let me in.* The modern *gospel* completely reinforces that idea, except for one small detail—very little preaching nowadays addresses eternity, heaven, and hell. Instead, it is all focused on having a good life in the here and now.

We must leave behind our slavish fear of not offending people and return to preaching the Gospel Jesus said His Spirit would anoint with conviction—only that Gospel will save! I do not mean to imply that there are no pastors out there who still preach the whole counsel of God. Nor do I mean to say there are no youth pastors with God's fire in their hearts who do not warn their youth with tears. However, I am absolutely persuaded the Gospel preached overall today is unquestionably *Gospel Lite* compared to the New Testament, or even the Gospel I heard preached more than twenty-five years ago when I first became a Christian.

It is not a matter of preaching *hell fire*, it is a matter of preaching the whole counsel of God. Only then will our hearers truly understand the entire nature and character of God. This is an enormous part of what is so tragically wrong with this generation of young people. The majority of them **do not** respect God as an authority figure. If they acknowledge Him at all, their perception of Him is often as a *big teddy bear in the sky* who would never judge them for their sin. They have little or no concept of Him as the sovereign Monarch of the universe before Whom they will stand on Judgment Day to give an account of their lives.

Currently, the *trendy message* is all about finding meaning and purpose in life, not repenting of sin, escaping God's judgment, or taking up your cross daily to follow Jesus. So many scandals involving church leaders, along with our anemic *self-help* message has made a mockery of God's authority in our society as a whole. It is having its most devastating affect on our Millennial Generation, creating not only blasphemous attitudes and actions, but a blasé response to the need to believe in Jesus. Perhaps worst of all, we have been guilty of removing one of God's key motivating agents of change—the fear of the Lord.

Chapter 20

No Fear!

As I speak to college students (even those raised in church) across America each year, I am still stunned at times by the blasphemous things they say. This generation likes *shock value*, so they think nothing of saying unimaginable things against the God of the Bible. It ranges from how *ludicrous and absurd* Jesus' claim to being the only way is, to the ways they are going to tell God a thing or two when they see Him. They even link vulgar sexual references to His Holy name just to show contempt. Their guilt before God is not even a viable issue for most of them. They surely don't know that judgment awaits those who have never received sin's pardon.

One phrase so accurately applies to this generation: ***There is no fear of God before their eyes (Romans 3:18).*** By omitting the harsher aspects of the Gospel from our message, we have created a generation who has no fear of God. At least in my generation we knew it existed. On the few occasions I did happen to hear a preacher talk about s*tanding before God on Judgment Day*, it definitely made an impression on me. When I was a teenager, the possibility of hell was very real and always in the back of my mind. I did fear God to some degree, but because I had no understanding of what it meant to be a Christian, I was a sinner. However, there were definitively things I would not do and places I would not go. There were sins I passed up because I thought twice about the eternal consequences. The kids I speak with on campus these days do not seem to be thinking twice about sin. The blasphemous things they say so often and so nonchalantly demonstrates they do not fear God. They say, *There is no heaven, there is no hell, there is only **now** for me!* And they live by that creed.

The vast majority of them, even the Christians, think the concept of *fearing God* is a joke, and they openly mock it. For many others, the concept of fearing God is a **hideous unspiritual** concept. Where do they get such an idea? Christians and even a great many preachers today marginalize the idea of fearing God. They say that term *only means* to reverence or respect God, not to actually fear Him. They say it is an invalid motive for turning to God. However, I find just the opposite is true when I look in the Bible; Proverbs 1:7 tells us only fools despise this concept! At least three times scripture declares the fear of the Lord to be the very beginning of wisdom.[1] One example: ***The fear of the Lord is the beginning of wisdom, and knowledge of the Holy One is understanding (Proverbs 9:10).***

As I looked into this concept of fearing God fresh and new, I was amazed at all the wonderful promises tied directly to it: long life, honor, wealth, and it is also directly linked to shunning and avoiding evil.[2] Perhaps the one we need most is ***he who fears the Lord has a secure fortress, and for his children it will be a refuge.***[3] It seems, according to God's Word, Christians and preachers should be maximizing, not minimizing, the idea of fearing God in their message. And what about the notion that fearing God ONLY means to reverence and is an invalid motive for turning to God?

Jesus said, *I will show you whom you should fear: Fear him who, after the killing of the body, has power to throw you into hell. Yes, I tell you, fear him (Luke 12:5).* He also used perhaps the most extreme words of His entire public ministry with this warning: *If your hand causes you to sin, cut it off. It is better for you to enter life maimed than with two hands to go into hell, where the fire never goes out. And if your foot causes you to sin, cut it off. It is better for you to enter life crippled than to have two feet and be thrown into hell. And if your eye causes you to sin, pluck it out. It is better for you to enter the kingdom of God with one eye than to have two eyes and be thrown into hell, where their worm does not die, and the fire is not quenched (Mark 9:43-48).*

From the lips of Jesus we certainly get the impression that fearing God is something that carries slightly more weight than just respecting God. Jesus obviously considered fearing God and eternity in hell very good motives to turn from sin and to God. However, none of this will ever fit into the category of inoffensive, positive, and upbeat.

As we have already discussed, it is well documented that evangelicals have by and large abandoned talking about hell. Many prominent evangelical theologians have completely dismissed the idea of hell altogether, or at least taken away its threat. They say that the concept of fire is strictly figurative. I am convinced by embracing this kind of anemic theology and shrinking back from declaring the full counsel of God in our preaching, we have short-circuited one of God's greatest tools of influence upon the unsaved. As a result of losing the fear of the Lord, our society and culture have become cancerously irreverent and our children are paying the highest price for this folly.

Furthermore, by doing so we are inadvertently sending multitudes of young people spilling over the precipice and into the abyss of hell. By forsaking God's law, never talking about judgment, and extinguishing the flames of hell (at least in our minds) we accomplish two things. One, we lessen, if not remove all together, our urgent concern for the lost. Secondly, we remove a legitimate scriptural incentive for the unsaved to turn from their sin and to God.

While many modern preachers neutralize the threat of a real lake of fire, the great preacher Charles Spurgeon articulately pointed out the exact result that feeble message will have when it comes into contact with human nature. He also left no room to doubt regarding his utter conviction of its reality:

> *Now, do not begin telling me that, that is metaphorical fire: who cares for that? If a man were to threaten to give me a metaphorical blow on the head, I should care very little about it; he would be welcome to give me as many as he pleased. And what say the wicked? "We do not care about metaphorical fires." But they are real, sir—yes, as real as yourself. There is a real fire in hell, as truly as you now have a real body—a fire exactly like that which we have on earth in everything except this—that it will not consume, though it will torture you.* – Charles H. Spurgeon [4]

Kindness and Severity?

I want to add an enormous qualifier at this juncture. While I firmly believe that the fear of God **is** the beginning of wisdom, it is by no means in my estimation the end of God's wisdom! **LOVE** is God's most preeminent and enduring attribute and the greatest motive for serving Him. It may also sound by this point that my understanding of God is one of an utter tyrant who delights in tossing sinners into the lake of fire. I assure you nothing could be further from the truth. We will visit the subject of God's tender kindness a little later.

The Apostle Paul made a very interesting statement in the Book of Romans. He said, **"Consider therefore the kindness and severity of God."** I think so few modern believers are ever exposed to this reality, that God is both kind and severe at the same time. *But how can that be?* we may ask. The New Living translation does a good job of defining that for us. *Notice how God is both kind and severe. He is severe toward those who disobeyed, but kind to you if you continue to trust in his kindness. But if you stop trusting, you also will be cut off (Romans 11:22 NLT).* Whether or not one experiences God's kindness or severity simply comes down to an individual's status with the Lord—his standing before God.

The New Testament distinction couldn't be more clear. If you are in a saving relationship with Jesus Christ of Nazareth, you will experience the most unimaginable divine kindness ever demonstrated to human kind. If you choose not to believe and *opt out* of His one and only plan of salvation, you will experience His severity for eternity. That is the focal point of all preaching found in the New Testament. In far too much of today's preaching that distinction is being lost. Instead it is being blurred into a muddy mixture that does not change hearts and lives. Bottom-line, our message **should** have a sobering effect on someone who is headed down the wrong road away from God. It is in many ways their only hope of redemption, and we dare not hesitate to preach the whole counsel of God. This generation desperately needs to hear that message.

I'm not advocating that we start every youth service by telling the kids they are going to hell. I'm certainly not suggesting that sin, repentance, and judgment are the only subjects we should preach. I personally preach on the cross more than any other single subject. In fact, every time I begin to speak to someone in a one-on-one conversation about the Gospel or begin to preach publicly to the lost, I am very purposefully heading toward one subject and one subject alone—the cross where Jesus Christ demonstrated the incomprehensible love of God. But, that is not the starting place; they must perceive their guilt before God before they will cry out to be saved. Then the message of a Savior and His blood-soaked cross will be the most beautiful words they will ever hear.

We must include all of God's message. It is akin to baking a cake. You have to have all the ingredients for it to taste right. We may think that sugar is the most important ingredient, but actually there is more flour involved than sugar. Although it would not taste right minus sugar, without flour it would not be a cake at all.

God has called us to dispense the Gospel to people. Our message is like the cake—love represents the sugar, repentance of sin is the flour, and God's judgment is the shortening. We now try to leave out two primary substances the Bible includes in the recipe, and we wonder why no one eats our cake. Just like a cake without flour would have no substance, the Gospel without the concepts of sin, judgment, and ultimate punishment if we reject the pardon, has no substance and no relevance.

A Message That Pierces the Heart

Preaching in the New Testament had a profound effect on its hearers; it was a message *with teeth,* more than just empty words. If we are preaching a truly Biblical message accompanied by the conviction of the Holy Spirit, we should see the same result. However, I am persuaded if we continue to preach an anemic *soft sell gospel* we will not make an impact on this generation.

On the day of Pentecost, Peter stood up and courageously declared the Gospel. The Bible records the result as he finished his message: ***"Therefore let all Israel be assured*** *of this: God has made this Jesus, whom you crucified, both Lord and Christ." When the people heard this, they were cut to the heart and said to Peter and the other apostles, "Brothers, what shall we do?" Peter replied, "Repent and be baptized, every one of you, in the name of Jesus Christ for the forgiveness of your sins. And you will receive the gift of the Holy Spirit" (Acts 2:36-38).*

Peter's preaching brought conviction, and the people were cut to the heart and cried out for an answer. To turn this generation of young people back to God, we must return to powerful preaching that addresses the real issue of the condition of their heart before God. So much preaching now sounds witty and sophisticated but it no longer has the scalpel-sharp edge of conviction. This was not the case when the first century church took their message to their world; it was accompanied with intense conviction.

Paul said, *Our gospel came to you not simply with words, but also with power, with the Holy Spirit and with deep conviction (1Thessalonians 1:5a).* That kind of preaching has the most powerful result of all—it pierces to the heart and creates real and lasting change and commitment. This is exactly what we so desperately need today—deep conviction! This alone can save multitudes in this generation. However, we dare not think it is a painless process. It is not the easiest to deliver, but I believe the souls of our young people are worth the effort.

To be honest, it has been a real struggle for me to include this topic in this book, but I felt it was absolutely necessary to address it in order to have any hope of turning this generation around. Paul apparently had to fight through some of his own misgivings when confronting the issue of sin and its serious consequences. In the end, he delivered the message that brought real spiritual change to a group of believers he loved. He beautifully articulates why it was so needed both then and now.

Even if I caused you sorrow by my letter, I do not regret it. Though I did regret it—I see that my letter hurt you, but only for a little while—yet now I am happy, not because you were made sorry, but because your sorrow led you to repentance. <u>For you became sorrowful as God intended and so were not harmed in any way by us. Godly sorrow brings repentance that leads to salvation and leaves no regret</u>, but worldly sorrow brings death (2 Corinthians 7:8-10 Emphasis added). He went on to say it produced earnestness and alarm. We too desperately need all these things.

Much like today, the Corinthian church found itself sinking into the quicksand of worldliness, grievous sin, and immorality. Paul, sensing the true life and death nature of the struggle going on, delivered a difficult message to bring deep repentance of sin. We call that message *First Corinthians* today. As difficult as it must have been, he said he did not regret it for it brought about the godly sorrow that led to repentance that leads to salvation!

My prayer is we will rediscover the message the early church preached. I pray that millions of lost young people will hear those words of eternal life, be pierced to the heart, experience godly sorrow that leads to repentance, fall on their knees before Jesus, and find God's forgiveness and salvation.

Chapter 21

His Mercy Endures to all Generations

Lost and Found

I can remember a few occasions when I was just a little boy, being in a huge department store with my parents. Something would suddenly catch my eye, usually some neat toy. I would stop in my tracks and then gravitate toward it. My parents would be looking at some *grown-up* stuff nearby. I would spend a few minutes mesmerized by whatever object had caught my eye. I was as happy as a lark one minute, playing with a plastic airplane, but suddenly something would not seem right.

I would come to myself and realize where I was and that I had been away from my parents too long. A quick glance up the aisle would confirm they were no longer standing where they had been when I so carelessly drifted away from them. I would race up the aisle to the corner where I could look in all directions; they were nowhere to be seen! Oh no! A surge of pure panic would seize me and my heart would begin to pound.

For the next minute or so I would frantically search the nearby aisles, my eyes hysterically scanning in all directions, looking for their familiar forms, to no avail. Three minutes of this brought sheer terror to my young mind, tears rolled down my cheeks, and the overwhelming regret—*why, oh, why had I been so foolish*? The neat toy was now the furthest thing from my mind. **I was lost!** I wanted my parents like nothing else in all the world. Those seemed like the scariest moments of my young life.

Rounding a corner in a dead run, suddenly I would see my mom and dad and all the adrenalin and fear would disappear in sweet relief. I would run headlong into their waiting arms. Normally, after they had calmed me down and hugged away the tears, a bit of scolding came my way. But I didn't care. I once was lost, but now I was found! The Bible uses many different words and concepts to describe man's separation from God. For me the one that seems to capture the essence of God's heart and nature best is lost. Jesus said that He had come to **seek** and **save** that which was lost.[1] This description best portrays not only our true condition, but God's attitude toward that circumstance.

I perceive this generation's situation to be truly dire, their peril is very real. They seem hopelessly lost, but are they beyond recovery? If we had to rely solely on human effort, it would be far too late. We can take inspiration from the true story of an inexperienced young missionary approaching a vast land of millions of lost unbelieving heathen. The first Protestant missionary sent to China was Robert Morrison in 1807. In route, the ship's owner tried to poke mockingly into the young missionary's confidence with the following question: "And so, Mr. Morrison, you really expect to make an impression on the idolatry of the great Chinese Empire?" But, Morrison was unruffled and replied, "No, sir, but I expect God will."[2]

Redemption

The greatest hope for this generation, indeed for every generation, is God's loving disposition. His nature reflected in His marvelous plan of redemption reveals both the tenderness of His heart and the indescribable lengths He will go to rescue us. If you have a Bible nearby as you are reading, I want to ask you to do something (if not, simply use your imagination). Open your Bible to Genesis, chapter one, and put your thumb there. Now turn to Genesis, chapter three, and insert your index finger. Notice you are grasping only one or two pages of actual Bible text between your thumb and finger.

Here in these first couple of chapters of Genesis, man is walking in sinless perfection with his Creator. He is completely unashamed in God's sweet presence and is enjoying an idyllic life in a garden paradise created just for him and his wife. However, it doesn't last long. If you simply consider the actual thickness of the pages between your thumb and finger you will note it is too thin to measure. In chapter three, we find the story of the fall of man. Sin enters the story! Man is now hiding from God and actually doing all he can to avoid contact with Him. He is driven from God's beautiful garden along with all the rest of us.

But amazingly, before he is even out of the garden, God kills an innocent animal and covers Adam and Eve's guilt and shame. Not just that, God immediately announced with perfect clarity His will and intention to redeem man back to Himself! Now insert your thumb in Genesis three, stretch your other fingers all the way to the end of your Bible, to the very end of Revelation. Now, you have the massive thickness of more than a thousand pages in your hand. If you have ever wanted to know what the message of the Bible really is, it is right in front of you. Those first one or two razor thin pages are how long mankind continued in that perfect sinless fellowship with God. The rest of that massive book is pulsating with one very simple message straight from God's very heart—**HE WANTS US BACK!!!**

Unlike Adam and Eve, the rest of us have never experienced that paradisiacal, perfect relationship with God; even so, we know about it instinctively. Although we have never been there, shadowy glimpses of Eden still linger in our consciousness. The Bible says God has set eternity in our hearts.[3] We are created in the image of God for one purpose alone, to walk with Him, experience Him, and to enjoy His company—and we long for it. Jesus said, *Now this is eternal life: that they may know you, the only true God, and Jesus Christ, whom you have sent (John 17:3).* He did not define eternal life in terms of an endless timetable, but rather in endless fellowship with God! He wants to ultimately restore us to that place of being able to walk with Him in sinless perfection again. He wants to bring us to a beautiful place that He has prepared just for us, where we can once again walk unashamedly in His sweet presence for all eternity.

This is not simply God's mission, **THIS IS GOD'S VERY NATURE!** This represents our greatest hope to see this generation of young people redeemed. We are not working against God in desiring the restoration of multitudes of young people; we are in perfect sync with His plan and character. He identifies us as His co-workers in this marvelous plan of redemption. As Christians, our very lives are simply instruments to sound out His master symphony. He has given us extraordinary promises, tools, and even weapons, all to accomplish His one great task—**REDEMPTION!** He invites us to join Him in His work. God wants to save and redeem our children more than we can imagine, but we need to give ourselves to Him in cooperation with His plan. Every day, every hour, every task, every dream, every priority, and all our resources, should be yielded to Him—put at His disposal in His plan of redemption.

The generation of young people currently living in the western world is as lost as any generation in history. They are as far from Eden as one can possibly be. They have bitten into the serpent's original seductive lies, *Did God really say? You will not surely die!* They are spiritually poisoned, along with the rest of humankind, and are on the broad road leading to destruction. But it is not too late! The very God of the universe desires to restore them and has gone to undreamed of lengths to bring them back to Himself. From the moment God found Adam and Eve cowering in shame after their sinful disobedience in the garden, He began the process of their spiritual restoration. He has never stopped redeeming us, His beloved creation, through thousands of years of human history.

The Old Testament's Merciful God!

Some at first glance may consider the Old Testament harsh. A superficial look does seem to reveal a God of judgment, but a closer look reveals the tender mercies of our God. He delights to save, not destroy. The most overwhelming and predominate aspects of His character are love, mercy, redemption, and forgiveness. He prefers and delights in showing mercy rather than judgment; that is His very nature!

Few people on earth have ever known God as intimately as Moses did. The Bible declares, *The Lord would speak to Moses face to face, as a man speaks with his friend (Exodus 33:11a).* In one of the most spectacular encounters any human being has ever experienced with God, He revealed Himself to Moses in an extremely tangible way. He sheltered Moses in the cleft of a rock. He then passed before him in glorious splendor and let His faithful servant see a glimpse of Him. As God did so, He proclaimed his Name and nature to Moses.

Then the Lord came down in the cloud and stood there with him, and proclaimed his name, the Lord. And he passed in front of Moses, proclaiming, "The Lord, the Lord, the compassionate and gracious God, slow to anger, abounding in love and faithfulness, maintaining love to thousands, and forgiving wickedness, rebellion and sin. Yet he does not leave the guilty unpunished (Exodus 34:5-7a). The first seven characteristics He lists about Himself are about His compassionate loving nature and His willingness to forgive sin, wickedness, and even rebellion.

However, if all these are rejected and people stubbornly resist His grace, He will eventually not let their guilt go unpunished. The wages of sin is death. Sooner or later sinners will pay for their rebellion against God. But even in that, God is not pleased but grieved. Notice God's ultimate desire for us shining through in the following two passages. *"As surely as I live," declares the Sovereign Lord, "I take no pleasure in the death of the wicked, but rather that they turn from their ways and live. Turn! Turn from your evil ways! Why will you die, O house of Israel?" (Ezekiel 33:11).*

This day...I have set before you life and death, blessings and curses. <u>Now choose life, so that you and your children may live</u> (Deuteronomy 30:19 Emphasis added).

Here we see that God truly gives man a choice in his morality. But, God is not satisfied to leave us with the choice; He influences us toward the good. He tells us plainly what He wants—for us to choose life! While it may be true the consequences of sin can wreak havoc for decades or even longer, God's mercy endures <u>FOREVER</u>. *For the Lord is good; His mercy is everlasting, and His truth endures to all generations (Psalm 100:5 NJKV).* What a glorious promise we have, that His mercy and truth endures to **ALL GENERATIONS**. God's enduring qualities are not of harshness, but of kindness. Through thousands of years of human history, God's goodness has been on display for anyone who would turn to Him. Despite wickedness beyond description, God is always ready to forgive and extend His mercy to those who will call on Him. This generation is certainly included in God's beautiful promise.

God's Matchless Concern for Humanity

Another Old Testament figure who understood well God's true nature in regard to lost humanity was Nehemiah. He declared, *But you are a forgiving God, gracious and compassionate, slow to anger and abounding in love. Therefore you did not desert them (Nehemiah 9:17b).* He virtually sums up in three short verses the entire Old Testament and God's dealings with Israel:

> *But they were disobedient and rebelled against you; they put your law behind their backs. They killed your prophets, who had admonished them in order to turn them back to you; they committed awful blasphemies. So you handed them over to their enemies, who oppressed them. But when they were oppressed they cried out to you. From heaven you heard them, and in your great compassion you gave them deliverers, who rescued them from the hand of their enemies.*
>
> *But as soon as they were at rest, they again did what was evil in your sight. Then you abandoned them to the hand of their enemies so that they ruled over them. And when they cried out to you again, you heard from heaven, and in your compassion you delivered them time after time (Nehemiah 9:26 -28).*

We in modern America are guilty of many of these same things: disobedience, rebellion, turning our backs on God's law, and committing awful blasphemies. We, like ancient Israel, are surrounded by a world full of enemies seething with hatred toward us. If God ever turns us over fully to them, 9/11 will seem small in comparison. Our best course of action is to call on God day and night for His mercy, because we deserve no better than Israel. Our hope also lies in what God put in the heart of those prophets of long ago, *who had admonished them in order to turn them back to you.*

God's primary message and purpose is always to turn people back to Him no matter how sinfully they have behaved. *Mercy triumphs over judgment (James 2:13b NKJV).* A beautiful example of that comes to us from the book of Jonah where this same pattern played itself out in Nineveh, the capital of the great Assyrian Empire. This city was idolatrous, immoral, and brutal beyond words. The Prophet Nahum later called it *the city of blood, full of lies and full of plunder.*[4] God pronounced a very specific Day of Judgment—in just forty days the city would be destroyed!

But, again God preferred mercy. He sent the unwilling prophet Jonah to warn the idolatrous pagans of their impending doom. Why would God care for these idol worshipping pagans with whom He had no covenant? Jonah certainly didn't care. After Jonah eventually preached his dire warning in the streets of this massive city, something miraculous happened. The wicked king living there knew what was at stake and he knew intuitively what God was looking for—repentance. *"Let everyone call urgently on God. Let them give up their evil ways and their violence. Who knows? God may yet relent and with compassion turn from his fierce anger so that we will not perish." When God saw what they did and how they turned from their evil ways, he had compassion and did not bring upon them the destruction he had threatened (Jonah 3:8b-10).*

After this glorious demonstration of God's mercy, goodness, and grace for the citizens of Nineveh, Jonah's bad attitude flared up once again. He was actually **upset** that God had not destroyed the city. God gave him an object lesson that once again revealed the magnitude of His saving mercy. On a hillside east of Nineveh, God used a vine and a worm to teach Jonah a profound lesson. During this encounter, in the closing verses of Jonah's short book, we find possibly one of scripture's greatest glimpses into the very heart of God:

> *But the Lord said, "You have been concerned about this vine, though you did not tend it or make it grow. It sprang up overnight and died overnight. But Nineveh has more than a hundred and twenty thousand people who cannot tell their right hand from their left, and many cattle as well. Should I not be concerned about that great city?" (Jonah 4:10-11).*

While Jonah was absolutely consumed with his comfort and the temporal, God revealed the passion of all heaven by declaring His love and concern over the lost condition of the people of Nineveh. God knew exactly how many souls would have perished in Nineveh—120,000. The high and lofty, holy King of heaven looked down on this wicked city and was so utterly compassionate that He even took note of the cattle living there. That Yahweh would show concern for this city demonstrates the magnitude and breadth of His saving mercy.

God was willing to forestall an already pronounced judgment for the sake of 120,000 lost souls. Oh, what hope this should give us considering the sad spiritual condition of America's youth culture. They, like the citizens of Nineveh, are sinful and hopelessly lost; the vast majority of kids in America do not know their right hand from their left when it comes to spiritual matters.

There are far, far more of them than the 120,000 who lived in the Assyrian capital. Like those citizens of Nineveh, if they turn from their rampant sexual immorality, idolatry, blasphemy contests, and their unbelief about Jesus, God will forgive them and lovingly embrace them. No matter how far they are from God right now, no matter how grievous their sin, God desires to redeem and restore their weary lost souls. That is His nature.

God in the Old Testament wanted to spare multitudes facing judgment. From Adam to Malachi, God's glorious voice of redemption was calling out to all those generations. I believe His voice is still calling out, ***Shall I not be concerned about this generation!***

Chapter 22

Finding the Lost Sheep

Despite the revelation of God's redeeming character, we must always realize salvation is not automatic! In Psalm 103, we find tender sweet promises about God's merciful nature. But notice the minimal prerequisite to experiencing God's mercy is to embrace the beginning of wisdom, which is the fear of the Lord. *The Lord is compassionate and gracious, slow to anger, abounding in love. He will not always accuse, nor will he harbor his anger forever; he does not treat us as our sins deserve or repay us according to our iniquities. For as high as the heavens are above the earth, so great is his love <u>for those who fear him</u>; as far as the east is from the west, so far has he removed our transgressions from us. As a father has compassion on his children, so the Lord has compassion on <u>those who fear him</u>; for he knows how we are formed, he remembers that we are dust (Psalm 103:8-14 Emphasis added).* I have noted that something of critical importance has been lost to this generation. The line of exactly who receives God's gracious pardon has been blurred beyond recognition for most modern young people.

They have not heard the full counsel of God declared and have a very basic misconception. They do not realize that even though God's love is unconditional, His forgiveness is NOT! For instance, 1 John 1:9 declares: *__IF WE CONFESS__ our sins, he is faithful and just and will forgive us our sins and purify us from all unrighteousness (Emphasis added)*. Confessing our sins is a condition. All the beauty and promise of eternal life found in John 3:16 is only for those who believe in Him! Believing in Him is a condition. In fact, the condition of **all conditions** repeated hundreds of times throughout the New Testament is we must believe in the Gospel of Jesus Christ. This perhaps sounds so utterly basic, but it has been lost in today's culture. Young people must be rescued from a *belief system* of UN-belief. Action is still required.

Almost my entire inspiration for writing this book came to me from the book of Ezekiel. After several years of ministry on college campuses here in America, I was gearing up for my next season. I was asking God to give me fresh heart before heading back to campus that next fall. That summer, He arrested my attention in a very special way when I read the thirty-fourth chapter of Ezekiel. Here God reveals from the depths of His very being the utter heartbreak of seeing lost sheep stray.

Through the prophet Ezekiel, God paints a tragic picture of sheep straying from His precious flock, wandering off in all directions and being devoured and torn apart by predators. **The very sadist portion** of the picture is that He laments over and over again that NO ONE IS SEARCHING OR LOOKING FOR HIS LOST SHEEP. He reiterates this same point eight different times in this short chapter. *__You have not brought back the strays or searched for the lost__ (Ezekiel 34:4b Emphasis added)*. How vividly this mirrors what is happening today to this generation of young people. They have been drifting tragically out the back door of the church for a long time now, and until very recently we all carried on as if nothing was happening. Thankfully, the time for *business as usual* is over and I am finally hearing other voices of concern.

I too must confess, for a time, I was more or less oblivious to what was happening. Although my ministry has primarily been focused on global missions and evangelism since 1984, I did pastor for three years in the mid-nineties. Our church always had as many teens as adults, and I tried to be faithful to watch over the flock and preach the full counsel of God. When our most spiritual young man left for college, I didn't think much about it. He was an extraordinary young man. He wrote worship songs, felt a call to serve, and generally seemed to take the things of God very seriously. I even kept in touch with him while he was attending school and visited him on campus a couple of times.

We talked about some of the issues he was grappling with, however, I did not sense the magnitude of his struggles until it was apparently too late. He experienced a total crisis of faith, and to my knowledge has never recovered. What I regret most is that I was not more deliberate and specific in preparing him for the spiritual minefield ahead of him while at college. He even attended a school of seemingly great Christian heritage, named after one of my greatest heroes of the faith, John Wesley. I had no idea what an **ANTI**-Christian agenda was awaiting him there. I still pray for him and wish I had been a better pastor for him as he headed off to college. This brings us to a rather uncomfortable subject, the context of Ezekiel 34.

One thing you learn as a preacher is to not take verses or passages out of context. However, I would prefer to do that with this particular text. It becomes unmistakable what is on God's mind with the opening verse of this chapter as He speaks clearly through His prophet: *The word of the Lord came to me: "Son of man, prophesy against the shepherds of Israel.*" [1] I'm not going to touch that with a *ten foot pole*; I have no desire, in a manner of speaking, to *prophesy against* pastors.

The only thing I would venture to say is this. If a senior pastor thinks this book is not for him, but rather only for the student minister or youth workers, I would have to disagree. That simply is not the case. We must address the current crisis at every level, from the parents and grandparents all the way to the senior pastor. How could anyone have a pastor's heart and not be deeply troubled about multitudes of youth leaving the back door of the church at graduation? Or not be utterly grieved about sheep who are going astray and being devoured by this world's anti-Christian belief system?

This passage of Ezekiel speaks to all of us who care about lost people and describes perfectly what is happening in our day and time. *You have not strengthened the weak or healed the sick or bound up the injured. <u>You have not brought back the strays or searched for the lost</u>... So they were scattered because there was no shepherd, and when they were scattered they became food for all the wild animals. <u>My sheep wandered over all the mountains and on every high hill. They were scattered over the whole earth, and no one searched or looked for them</u> (Ezekiel 34:4-6 Emphasis added).*

God essentially says the same thing over and over again throughout the chapter. He leaves us no possible room to misunderstand what has grieved Him so deeply—stray sheep for whom no one is searching. I cannot help but apply this to our modern context. Young people who are leaving the church at eighteen (especially those going off to college or the military) are particularly vulnerable to attack. God says that as these sheep get scattered, they literally become food for all the wild animals. Nowhere is that more true than for those going off to a secular state university. The pack of ferocious humanistic predators waiting there could not be more dangerous to an eighteen year old away from family and church for the first time. I have spent the last few years looking at the gaping wounds inflicted on the souls of these former youth group kids by the God-hating wolves hiding behind the higher educational system.

Parents, pastors, and churches must take Ezekiel's words to heart and do all we can to strengthen the weak and bind up the injured as quickly as possible. We must resist the *out-of-sight out-of-mind* trap of the enemy. We must not let them fall through the cracks at graduation. We must not let them wander into the dangerous hills of adulthood alone. Furthermore, we must go out and search and do all we can to bring them back before they are completely devoured by the ruthless enemy of their souls.

On a practical level, I believe as the church we must be very deliberate to prepare them for the realities of modern universities. Before they ever leave, we must address the issues they will face in the secular, liberally lop-sided class-room. We must develop materials with basic apologetics that are interesting and effective for their age group. We must help them to realize the rock solidness of the Christian faith. We must especially build a solid foundation of the integrity and reliability of God's Word, for this comes under attack virtually every day at modern universities. We must create a better way of keeping up with them while they are geograph-ically hundreds of miles away at school. We must do every-thing possible to not let them become isolated.

We cannot leave it up to them to find a church or Christian group at their campus, but we must exhort and assist them in that process. I realize at that stage they are young adults and making their own decisions, but we must help them to under-stand how high the stakes are and how dangerous the envi-ronment really is they are entering. We must communicate to them how hazardous it is to become isolated at that critical season of their life. I believe our churches must purposefully build a hedge of protection through prayer around our youth groups, especially those graduating and heading away geographically.

Sheep are largely oblivious to danger. By the time a sheep realizes it is in danger it is too late; it is defenseless. The predator is too fast and too strong. That is why they must be kept together. That is why they need to be near the shepherd. That is why finding lost sheep is so crucial. That is why I have written this book.

Before I leave these practical ideas, let me say, I clearly understand that this is not an exact science. I know many people who have seemingly done everything right in raising their children, and yet they go astray. Thankfully, we have wonderful assurance from the Word of God for them. *Train a child in the way he should go, and when he is old he will not turn from it (Proverbs 22:6).* More than anything else this book is a wake-up call to make sure we are doing all that we possibly can as Christian families and churches to protect our children from this world's system.

In verse ten of Ezekiel 34, God turns a corner and stops talking about **our** responsibility and declares **His** ultimate plan for His precious flock. In a series of statements, He then begins to unfold His glorious plan of redemption:

∞ *I will rescue my flock from their mouths.*
∞ *I myself will search for my sheep.*
∞ *I will rescue them from all the places where they were scattered.*
∞ *I will search for the lost and bring back the strays.*[2]

He closes the passage with this sweet verse, *You my sheep, the sheep of my pasture, are people, and I am your God, declares the Sovereign Lord (Ezekiel 34:31).* The God of the Old Testament is not harsh. It is not difficult to find the tenderness with which He regards us, His creation. I call your attention to an especially appropriate verse for young people and those who love them.

He tends his flock like a shepherd: He gathers
the lambs in his arms and carries them close to
his heart; he gently leads those that have young.
Isaiah 40:11

Chapter 23

Jesus, the Good Shepherd

Nowhere was God's mercy more on display than in the person of Jesus of Nazareth. He is the hope of all mankind; God's ultimate plan of redemption, the Messiah! He is the reason we have assurance that this generation of youth can be redeemed. God kept His promise to search for the lost and bring back the strays. He sent Jesus as the Good Shepherd! He left the pure Holy glory of heaven and came down to this planet and got His feet dirty. He came and found the lowliest lost sinners. Jesus characterized His mission this way, *For the Son of Man came to seek and to save what was lost (Luke 19:10).*

On His mission to search for the lost sheep and to bring back the strays, Jesus had to go where they were. He came into contact with sinners and this angered the Jewish religious leaders of His day. Jesus' answer not only silenced them, it gave us one of the most beautiful and concise descriptions of His ministry found anywhere.

Now the tax collectors and "sinners" were all gathering around to hear him. But the Pharisees and the teachers of the law muttered, "This man welcomes sinners and eats with them." Then Jesus told them this parable: "Suppose one of you has a hundred sheep and loses one of them. Does he not leave the ninety-nine in the open country and go after the lost sheep until he finds it? And when he finds it, he joyfully puts it on his shoulders and goes home. Then he calls his friends and neighbors together and says, 'Rejoice with me; I have found my lost sheep.' I tell you that in the same way there will be more rejoicing in heaven over one sinner who repents than over ninety-nine righteous persons who do not need to repent" (Luke 15:1-7).

Obviously, the heart of Jesus is to search for the lost sheep until He finds them. This generation is truly full of those lost sheep! My prayer is in our day and time, He will find multitudes in this generation and joyfully put them on His shoulders and carry them home. However, it doesn't take multitudes returning to God to cause a celebration in heaven. Nothing else in scripture indicates that all of heaven rejoices over any other occurrence, but heaven erupts in joyful celebration over one sinner who repents. What a marvelous Savior! What a marvelous mission — to find lost sheep!

I am fully persuaded that despite the fact that literally millions of young people are lost in the western cultures alone (and millions more around the world), none of them are beyond His reach and care. In Matthew's version of this text, he includes an additional sentence from Jesus' words: *In the same way your Father in heaven is not willing that any of these little ones should be lost (Matthew 18:14).*

Both the Apostles Paul and Peter echoed this great confidence in the reach of God's offer of salvation and mercy: *This is good, and pleases God our Savior, who wants all men to be saved and to come to a knowledge of the truth*

(1 Timothy 2:3-4). He is patient with you, not wanting anyone to perish, but everyone to come to repentance (2 Peter 3:9b).

The Bible declares Jesus to be *the radiance of God's glory and the exact representation of his being (Hebrews 1:3a).* His life communicates to us the depth of God's love and concern for the lost.

Nowhere is this more clearly demonstrated than His sacrificial death on the cross. Jesus said, *I am the good shepherd. The good shepherd lays down his life for the sheep (John 10:11).* His death on the cross was not the product of the Jewish religious leaders' jealousy, nor of the brutal Roman justice system, but rather a completely calculated decision based on God's eternal goodness and love. *I lay down my life — only to take it up again. No one takes it from me, but I lay it down of my own accord (John 10:17b-18a).*

We must tell this generation that the God of Christianity cares so infinitely about them that He sent His own Son to live and die to rescue them. The Bible says, *This is how we know what love is: Jesus Christ laid down his life for us (1 John 3:16a).* The nature of crucifixion is far more brutal than our minds can imagine. He knew that in advance, but He valued the souls of this generation so much that He laid down His life on that torturous Roman cross to save every precious young person alive today.

I offered my back to those who beat me, my cheeks to those who pulled out my beard; I did not hide my face from mocking and spitting.[1] He took nails through His hands and His feet. He was savagely beaten, stripped, and mocked so their sins could be forgiven. He was wounded for their transgressions. He was bruised for their iniquities; the punishment that brought them peace was upon Him! The Bible says, *His appearance was so disfigured beyond that of any man and his form marred beyond human likeness.*[2]

Our young people have been bought with a price, and what a staggering cost it was! Jesus said, *Greater love has no one than this, that he lay down his life for his friends (John 15:13)*. That is the message they so desperately need to hear! That is the message that so radically transformed my life as a mixed-up seventeen year old. *For Christ did not send me to baptize, but to preach the gospel—not with words of human wisdom, lest the cross of Christ be emptied of its power. For the message of the cross is foolishness to those who are perishing, but to us who are being saved it is the power of God (1 Corinthians 1:17-18).*

I am fully persuaded that the message of the cross can turn around any generation. I am fully persuaded it can turn around **this** generation!

He himself bore our sins in his body on the tree, so that we might die to sins and live for righteousness; by his wounds you have been healed. For you were like sheep going astray, but now you have returned to the Shepherd and Overseer of your souls (1 Peter 2:24-25).

The Ministry of Reconciliation

God has overwhelmingly demonstrated His desire to save lost humanity, but more specifically, every young person in this current generation. Jesus, the Good Shepherd, has come to search for the lost sheep of this and every generation. Even though He already purchased their redemption on His cross, there remains more to do. We must spread the Word to this generation.

I mentioned earlier, one of the most profound moments in my walk with God was when I discovered that He has identified us as His fellow workers in His plan of redemption. *All this is from God, who reconciled us to himself through Christ and gave us the ministry of reconciliation: that God was reconciling the world to himself in Christ, not counting men's sins against them. And he has committed to us the message of reconciliation (2 Corinthians 5:18-19).*

For reasons incomprehensible to me, God has invited us, mere human beings, to participate in His great eternal epic. So here we are in what must surely be Act III in that drama. In America, a new generation of kids is in desperate need of being reconciled to God. The passage above indicates that the Kingdom is not on autopilot; we have been entrusted to carry out the vital ministry of reconciliation. Even though God has sent Jesus into this vast multitude of lost sheep called humanity – even though He has already died to save them – it remains unfinished until this Millennial Generation connects with that reality in a real and vital way by hearing the message.

The Apostle Paul said it so perfectly: *How, then, can they call on the one they have not believed in? And how can they believe in the one of whom they have not heard? And how can they hear without someone preaching to them? (Romans 10:14).* After looking at multitudes of harassed and helpless lost souls, Jesus said they were like *sheep without a shepherd.* He then told us exactly what needed to happen to rescue them. *The harvest is plentiful but the workers are few. Ask the Lord of the harvest, therefore, to send out workers into his harvest field (Matthew 9:37b-38).* Laborers must go into the midst of this harassed and helpless generation and tell them that God wants to bring their souls back to Himself. God has committed to us the ministry and message of reconciliation and we must be faithful to carry it out.

Man the Lifeboats!

We must all volunteer as God's fellow workers to rescue this generation; it is all-hands-on-deck! I have often used the example of a catastrophically damaged ocean liner to illustrate the nature of the ministry of reconciliation. After all, Jesus Himself called us to be fishers of men! Imagine a *special spring break cruise.* Aboard the massive gleaming white ship are thousands of young people, and you are on board as a chaperone.

After midnight, something goes tragically wrong! The huge vessel is listing and in trouble in a dangerous sea. Some of the more careless kids have already tumbled overboard and into the water. They are thrashing helplessly in the foaming surf, but they can't last long. Many more are clinging tenaciously to the rails and decks as the ship is sinking. But, tragically, most of the young people are asleep below and are completely oblivious to the growing danger.

Water is now pouring into the ship. The captain, absolutely convinced of the hopeless condition of the ship, calls for every able-bodied person to help get the young passengers in the lifeboats. It is time to evacuate the ship because those left on board will perish and sink into the cold dark waters below. What will you do? Will you join the rescue effort or stand idly by while so many young lives are being lost? The *S.S. Next Generation* **IS** sinking.

I feel overwhelmed by the sheer magnitude of what is happening to a generation of young people right before my eyes. Like Paul I cry out, "Who is equal to such a task?" [3] I realize as I walk onto a campus, I cannot save them. But the message of Jesus can! My goal is to reach my hand out to all I can and pull them from the dark turbulent waters that is secular culture today.

The words of Jude 23 apply: ***Snatch others from the fire and save them!*** Jesus, the Captain of our salvation, the Good Shepherd, has called us to be co-laborers together with Him in the ministry of reconciliation. We must answer His call! Perhaps you too feel helpless, overwhelmed, and wonder what you can do to make a difference in the lives of the next generation.

Breath from Heaven

Long, long ago the Spirit of God moved upon an ancient prophet named Ezekiel and brought him into a vast valley. As he lifted his eyes he beheld what must have been a stunning scene. There, stretched before him, the entire valley was filled with dead dry human bones. As he walked back and forth through the midst of this ghastly landscape, he was struck by the vast number of those long since slain, and also by their chalky dry lifelessness. He too must have felt very overwhelmed!

Then the Spirit of God asked him the most amazing question, *Son of man, can these bones live?* [4] Understandably hesitant and uncertain, the prophet said, *O Sovereign Lord, you alone know.*[5] Then God began a discourse that could only have been interpreted as a resounding Yes! God said to his startled prophet, *Prophesy to these bones, and say to them, "O dry bones, hear the word of the Lord! Thus says the Lord God to these bones: 'Surely I will cause breath to enter into you, and you shall live. I will put sinews on you and bring flesh upon you, cover you with skin and put breath in you; and you shall live. Then you shall know that I am the Lord.'"* [6]

Emboldened, the prophet did as he was told and prophesied to the entire valley of brittle dry bones! Remarkably, Ezekiel suddenly began to hear a noise, the sound of rattling as the bones started coming together! Next sinew, flesh, and skin covered them. But still they lay dead and motionless. Sadly, there was no breath in them; the miracle was yet incomplete.

Prophesy to the breath, he was told. *Prophesy, son of man, and say to the breath. "Thus says the Lord God:*

'Come from the four winds, O breath, and breathe on these slain, that they may live.'"[7] Again the prophet complied and did what he was told. The corpses began to stir and stood to their feet, an exceedingly great army!

As the wide eyed prophet stood marveling at what he had just witnessed, God explained to him that *These bones are the whole house of Israel*, who had said, *Our bones are dried up and our hope is gone; we are cut off.* [8] Even in the midst of our current situation we do not need to be hopeless. From this awesome story we learn that nothing is too hard for our God! He can bring a generation back from the dead and turn them into a vast exceedingly great army!

There are other lessons to be learned also; even though God had a miraculous recovery in mind, the bones still needed to hear the Word of the Lord! Not only that, God required Ezekiel's obedience. He ordered him to speak His word into what truly seemed like a bleak and impossible situation. Furthermore, even after the dry bones miraculously came together and were covered in sinew and flesh, they remained lifeless. God had to breathe on them to actually bring them back to life. So too, we must pray for the mighty rushing wind of the Holy Spirit to breathe on our generation and anoint our preaching.

However, we can do so with the glorious assurance that we are not alone in this struggle. God has already set in motion His timeless plan of redemption. His mercy and truth endure to **ALL GENERATIONS**. Don't be dismayed, for there is much evidence that He is already working mightily in their midst!

Chapter 24

Signs of Life

Seven Thousand Who Have Not Yet Bowed Their Knee to Baal!

In early 2003, my wife and I were just beginning to grasp the overwhelming spiritual attack against America's youth. We knew the sad and alarming statistics, but closer to home we had seen firsthand some of the strongest youth we knew completely backslide while at university. We had just tasted our first college campus ministry and looked into the desolate faces of thousands of students without the knowledge of Jesus. We had heard with our own ears what seemed like unthinkable blasphemy and rebellion against God.

As we formed plans to shift a significant amount of our time and resources to reach out to this lost generation, we needed encouragement. The enormity of the task of actually helping turn this generation around seemed crushing. We knew God was leading us to care deeply about them and to do all we could to make a real difference. With close to 95% of kids raised in church by Christian parents leaving the faith while away at college, it almost seemed too late.

Then in February of that same year, we went to the nearby city of Waco to hear a friend speak. It just so happened to be Super Bowl Sunday and we started feeling sorry for him. His service would be competing with the biggest sports spectacle on the U.S. calendar! At least we would be there to support him, since he would probably have a very small crowd.

We had a little trouble finding the church, and as we rounded the last corner, we saw a huge parking lot cram packed! We entered the door of the sanctuary; the lights were low and the service was about to start. A very energetic worship band took the stage. Soon thousands of young people were worshipping the Lord with their hands and faces lifted to heaven. Others knelt in the aisles. As it turned out, we had walked into the closing service of a three-day missions conference called *World Mandate*, hosted by Antioch Community Church. Our friend's message was very moving and the service was heavenly.

As we were driving home, still aglow with the scene we had just beheld—thousands of young people worshipping Jesus with a passion and surrender I had not seen anywhere in decades—we knew God had arranged for us to be there. We felt like the old Prophet Elijah emerging from his cave of gloom and despair. It was as if God was saying the same thing to us: *I reserve seven thousand in Israel—all whose knees have not bowed down to Baal (1 Kings 19:18a).* It was our first realization that even though this generation still desperately needs a major turnaround, God has a remnant among them—a remnant that could potentially usher in a worldwide awakening on a scale not seen in two centuries.

Global Revival in Our Generation!!!

We have not missed this annual conference since. Every year Becky and I spend three days filling our spiritual fuel tank in Waco, surrounded by three thousand precious young people. It provides the perfect antidote to all the days we spend on campus dealing with irreverent young people. I acknowledge that much of this book paints a rather bleak picture, but now we are witnessing the possible beginnings of a global revival being sparked by this very age bracket. How can a generation be perishing and a global revival be happening at the same time?

I believe God is simply helping us discern what has probably always been the case—the contrast between these two factors. Of course, in every generation there has always been unsaved young people. And there has always been a segment of teens who have grown up in church who were uncommitted—those who were just going through the motions. However, in this generation, because of the two extremes, we are merely able to see it more clearly. As the darkness gets darker, the lights are simply shining all the brighter.

In times past, culture and society itself would not have tolerated the sacrilegious conduct that is now the norm at the college level. With almost no parental influence, no connection to the youth group at their *parent's church,* the true picture of what is in their hearts clearly emerges. As behavioral barriers in society have been lowered, kids no longer feel the need to be on their *artificial* best behavior. What is gone is the *squishy soft,* uncommitted middle. In such darkness, the teens who truly love God shine like beacon lights.

With the muddy mixture in the middle now dissipating, things have become more black and white. What has emerged is a statistically massive group who are lost and unsaved. They have no interest in following the Lord Jesus; they live purely for their fleshly self-gratification. There is also now a small super-committed remnant who love Jesus with an absolute burning passion. The lukewarm kids in-between feel no societal pressure to act Christian.

What gives me hope, that the seedling of global revival is already germinating in young hearts around the world, is the two defining passions that seem to be beating in the heart of this remnant. The first one is God-centered worship.

Worship

About a year after our *World Mandate* experience, we were visiting friends near Houston. The first night we were there, they just happened to be going to a concert at First Baptist Church of Houston. We drove downtown, parked, and walked into the huge facility. We sat in the balcony, only a few rows from the top. Even though we were far from the platform, the seats provided a very interesting vantage point to see something truly awesome.

Stretched before us in the packed arena-like atmosphere were about 4,500 young people worshipping Jesus, heart and soul! It seemed like every single one of them had their hands lifted heavenward to God. At other times, the floor of First Baptist Houston was jumping with a multitude of young worshippers dancing before the Lord with all their might like King David of old. It turns out the *concert* we were attending was actually a worship gathering, one stop on Louie Giglio's *Passion Tour*. Not only that, he has hosted spectacular *One-Day* events where literally tens of thousands of young people gather to worship Jesus open-air.

Even if this lively new manner of worship is not your *cup of tea*, I recommend you keep an open mind. Be careful not to dismiss it too quickly simply because of the youthful enthusiasm and musical style at its forefront. Even those of you who do not enjoy worship of this intensity should examine the substance of it to see what God might be doing. The Apostle Paul wrote, *I want men everywhere to lift up holy hands in prayer (1 Timothy 2:8a).* This is exactly what is happening in this generation.

When David brought the Ark back to Jerusalem, his wife, Michal, was quick to criticize her husband for dancing with such abandon in front of lowly slave girls. Not only did God chastise her by making her barren until the day of her death, David's response was less than apologetic and serves as an example for us today: *I will celebrate before the Lord. I will become even more undignified than this, and I will be humiliated in my own eyes. But by these slave girls you spoke of, I will be held in honor (2 Samuel 6:21b-22).* This man, David, who God Himself called a man after His own heart, gave us the following exhortations:

> *Praise him for his acts of power;*
> *praise him for his surpassing greatness.*
> *Praise him with the sounding of the trumpet,*
> *praise him with the harp and lyre,*
> *praise him with tambourine and dancing,*
> *praise him with the strings and flute,*
> *praise him with the clash of cymbals,*
> *praise him with resounding cymbals.*
> *Let everything that has breath praise the Lord.*
> *Praise the Lord.*
> *Psalm 150:2-6*

Here the King of Israel shows us that quiet reserved worship is not the only form that is acceptable to God. The boisterous sound of trumpets and the resounding clash of symbols, along with joyful dancing, apparently blesses God's heart as well. This generation responds to the expressive passion created in this kind of worship environment. I have worshipped with them for hours upon hours and I am convinced they are a delight to the very heart of Jesus! Again, King David's words confirm this idea:

> *Let the people of Zion be glad in their King.*
> *Let them praise his name with dancing and make music to him*

> *with tambourine and harp.*
> *For the Lord takes <u>delight</u> in his people.*
> *Psalm 149:2b-4a (Emphasis added)*

Worship saturates us with the Holy presence of God like no other earthly activity. As I have worshipped beside this remnant for the past several years at *World Mandate*, I have seen their remarkable devotion demonstrated toward God. At times their worship has all the raw energy, intensity, and abandon of rock and roll, minus the rebellion. The songs and spirit of the music is instead all about surrender to God. Some dance with a pure beautiful joy in worship of Jesus their King! But, there is a tender sweet quality present also. As the lyrics exalt and lift up Jesus, many of them fall to their knees in adoration of Him Who was crucified. Still others melt completely in devotion and lay on their faces on the concrete floor of the convention center, crying out to God, willing to be sent anywhere He directs.

Throughout the conference the services last three to four hours, most of it spent in worship. However, they also love God's Word and sit in rapt attention for lengthy powerful sermons. These are not man-centered, self help messages, but rather compelling exhortations to love God more and to pour out our lives in the service of His Kingdom. But perhaps the most remarkable aspect of this beautiful sovereign move of God's Spirit is where it leads. It is not simply a love of *goose bump* emotional experiences as in other movements. Indeed, it leads these young worshippers as far away from a pseudo-spiritual self-centered experience as possible. Instead, they eagerly offer themselves as living sacrifices to spread the message of Jesus to the world. This brings us to the second defining passion leading to global revival—missions.

World Missions

Paul called the generation who lived on the earth during his ministry crooked and depraved.[1] But he commended his young helper, Timothy, glowingly to the Philippian Church in the very personal letter to them: *I have no one else like him, who takes a genuine interest in your welfare. For everyone looks out for his own interests, not those of Jesus Christ. But you know that Timothy has proved himself, because as a son with his father he has served with me in the work of the gospel (Philippians 2:20-22).* Obviously, Timothy had the rare and extraordinary quality of being interested in what **JESUS** Himself was interested in.

Paul clearly defined this as the <u>*work of the Gospel!*</u> Timothy desired to lay down his life for the welfare of those in Philippi, by laboring in the Gospel. We must remember Timothy was not a native of this region. In modern terms, he had a passion for world missions!

That is the other defining characteristic of this glorious remnant God is raising up. During every service at *World Mandate*, they pray and intercede for the lost around the world. I have seen them streaming forward by the hundreds, if not thousands, to commit themselves to serve Jesus in the nations of the earth. It is not just *talk* brought on by the enthusiastic worship and preaching; they actually go to places where their lives are literally on the line!

I have had the privilege of hearing their testimonies of serving in places like Indonesia, Algeria, Morocco, Tunisia, Iraq, and Afghanistan! With glowing faces they testify of Jesus to people in hostile countries where it is forbidden. What is so extraordinary is the young people of this generation are fellow companions with the brave Christians of the first century. The same testimony could be said of today's remnant of zealous young people, as those early believers, *They overcame him by the blood of the Lamb and by the word of their testimony, and they did not love their lives to the death (Revelation 12:11 NKJV).*

With joyful hearts, they endure bone-jarring travel, hard work, weariness, culture shock, loneliness, and hardship for the Gospel. They eat unfamiliar, often disgusting food, live in rough unsanitary conditions and literally lay down their lives for Jesus Christ. How inspiring to have met extraordinary young women like Heather Mercer and Dana Curry—to have worshipped beside them and heard their testimonies of God's unfailing love. They have truly experienced His miraculous assistance while serving Jesus joyfully, even in a Taliban prison in Afghanistan. And, there are many, many others just like them, loving un-reached people in every nook and cranny of the world.

Loving a Generation

Amazingly, God has sovereignly raised up this generation of young people for such a time as this. The defining characteristics of this remnant are potent tools in the hands of the Lord of the harvest, and offer very real hope for worldwide youth revival. I cannot hide my love and admiration for these young people who worship Jesus so unashamedly and who so willingly lay down their lives to obey His command to take the Gospel to the ends of the earth! Getting to know them has been one of the richest experiences of my life.

I also love every prodigal, former youth group kid I meet out on the college campuses where I preach. I am overwhelmed by the spiritual peril they face. I believe they are carelessly losing their souls, exchanging the truth of God for lies, and being swallowed up by the voracious predator of sin. I cry out continually for the heart of Jesus, the Good Shepherd, to motivate me to go out and look for these lost sheep. And, I love the millions of completely lost, never-churched kids who have been completely blinded by the worst in modern culture. I pray that God will saturate my heart with a compassion that moves me to action, and to prayer, on their behalf. I also hope that as you have read this book, God has stirred your heart to care and care deeply about the multitudes in the valley of decision in this generation.

Jesus said we must work while it is day, for night is coming when no one can work.[2] We must rightly comprehend that any further complacency will be devastating and possibly irreparable in this defining moment of history for the Millennial Generation. We must truly perceive the danger and develop a sense of urgency. We must teach our children. We must suspend business as usual and consecrate ourselves to God in a special way. We must fast and pray. We must call on God to have an outpouring of His Spirit—a sweeping mighty revival in our churches, student ministries, youth groups, homes, and our hearts! We must not stop there but pray that the revival then becomes a full-blown awakening in our whole youth culture. We must recognize that nothing less will save the soul of this generation!

Notes

Chapter 1: Multitudes, Multitudes in the Valley of Decision!

1. *2005 Civil Unrest in France*, Wikpedia.com, various sources.
2. CBN News, January 9, 2007.
3. Author unknown, "College Sex," *Christianity Today*, September 1991, 17. As quoted in Billy Beacham, *Passion for Purity* Leader Guide (Fort Worth, Texas: Student Discipleship Ministries, 2000) 8. (Note from author: I believe since the survey was completed in 1991, the 17% of girls who believe sex before marriage is wrong has surely dropped even more as our culture has further eroded.)
4. ABC Network *20/20*, March 2, 2007.
5. Ibid.
6. Josh McDowell, *The Last Christian Generation* (Holiday, Florida: Green Key Books, 2006).
7. Ibid. 15.

Chapter 2: Finding a Lost Sense of Urgency

1. Martha T. Moore and Dennis Cauchon, "Delay meant death on 9/11," *USA Today*, September 3, 2002, 1.

2. Matthew 5:13-14.
3. Saying made popular by a book published in the sixties by Thomas A. Harris, *I'm OK, You're OK*, (New York: Harper & Row, 1969).
4. Matthew 7:13.

Chapter 3: What They Really Think

1. Psalm 95:7b-8a.
2. Matthew 12:34b (NKJV).
3. McDowell, *The Last Christian Generation*, 13.
4. Ron Luce, "Ron Luce Announces the Battle Cry," www.battlecry.com/pages/news3.php, accessed on March 14, 2007.
5. 2 Corinthians 10:4 (NKJV).

Chapter 4: Lower Education

1. Dave Eggers, Ninive Calegari, and Daniel Moulthrop, "Reading, Writing, Retailing," *New York Times*, June 27, 2005. As quoted in Ann Coulter, *Godless: The Church of Liberalism* (New York: Crown Forum, Crown Publishing Group, 2006), 160.
2. 1 Corinthians 15:33 (HCSB).
3. Coulter, *Godless*, 149.
4. Ibid. 182.
5. Erica E. Goode, "Communicating the Basic Facts Is Hard Enough: AIDS Makes It Even Tougher," *U.S. News & World Report*, November 16, 1987. As quoted in Coulter, *Godless*, 180.
6. Genesis 3:1
7. J. Dunphy, "A Religion for a New Age," *The Humanist*, Jan-Feb 1983, 23, 26.

8. Quoted from news story "Textbook Hearings" at the Texas State Board of Education, WFAA Channel 8 News, Dallas, Texas, September 8, 2004.

9. 1 John 2:18.

Chapter 5: Higher Education—the Graveyard of Belief

1. Jered T. Ede, "Deepthroating Hopkins: How Your Tuition Hike Pays the Gay Porn Industry," www.tcrecord.com/deepthroatinghopkins.htm, accessed on March 15, 2007.

2. Gayle Rubin in "Thinking Sex: Notes for a Radical Theory of the Politics of Sexuality," in *The Lesbian and Gay Studies Reader*, eds. Henry Abelove, Michele Aina Barale, and David Halperin (New York: Routledge 1993) 7. As quoted in Daniel J. Flynn, *Intellectual Morons: How Ideology Makes Smart People Fall For Stupid Ideas* (New York: Three Rivers Press, Crown Publishing Group, 2004), 52.

3. Quoted in Walter Williams, "Average Americans vs. Environmentalists" (March 2003), www.gmu.edu/departments/economics/wew/articles/fee/average.html, accessed on September 1, 2003. As quoted in Flynn, *Intellectual Morons*, 58.

4. Peter Singer, *Rethinking Life and Death: The Collapse of Our Traditional Ethics* (New York: St. Martin's Griffin, 1999), 130. As quoted in Flynn, *Intellectual Morons*, 74.

5. Peter Singer, "Heavy Petting," www.nerve.com/Opinions/Singer/heavyPetting/main.asp, accessed on March 14, 2001. As quoted in Flynn, *Intellectual Morons*, 76.

6. Quoted in Kushanava Choudhury, "Despite Rallies, University Defends Singer's Appointment to Faculty," *Daily Princetonian*, July 19, 1999, 1. As quoted in Flynn, *Intellectual Morons*, 77.

7. *Comedy and Tragedy: College Course Descriptions and What They Tell Us About Higher Education* (Herndon, VA: Young America's Foundation, 2003), 77. Eric Langborgh, "X-Rated Academia," *Campus Report,* March 2000, 1 "Spring Semester 2000: LGBT Related Courses," www.oberlin.edu/stuorg/LGBCC/spr2000. htm, accessed on March 2, 2004. As quoted in Flynn, *Intellectual Morons*, 21.
8. 27 News (ABC) "UW Felon Still Working On Campus," September 19, 2005, www.wkowtv.com/index. php/news/story/p/pkid/22256.
9. Marvin Olasky, "Conformity on Campus" *World Magazine*, December 18, 2004, Vol. 19, No. 49.
10. Vigen Guroian, "Dorm Brothel" *Christianity Today,* February 2005. Vigen Guroian is professor of theology at Loyola College in Baltimore. (Note from author: I learned of this novel, *I Am Charlotte Simmons*, by Tom Wolfe in this article and have not personally read it. The article stated that the book was full of graphic sexual content and profanity.)
11. Ibid.
12. Ibid.

Chapter 6: Re-education Camps

1. Flynn, *Intellectual Morons*, 99-100,106.
2. "Threatening Freshman 101," www.thefire.org.
3. Bernard Goldberg, *110 People Who Are Screwing Up America* (New York: Harper, 2006), 112-113.
4. Paul Strand, "The New Radicals: How Liberal Campuses Harass Conservatives," www.CBN.com, accessed March 24, 2007.
5. Ibid.
6. Ibid.
7. Ibid.

8. Ahmad Al-Qloushi, "Dissident Arab Gets the Treatment," FrontPageMagazine.com, January 6, 2005.
9. Strand, "The New Radicals."

Chapter 7: A Legion of Atheistic Professors Await!

1. Howard Kurtz, "College Faculties A Most Liberal Lot, Study Finds, *Washington Post*, Tuesday, March 29, 2005, page C01
2. Olasky, "Conformity on Campus"
3. Debra Johanyak, "Taking God to College," *On Mission*, Fall 2004. (Debra Johanyak, Ph.d., is a professor, author and playwright).
4. Olasky, "Conformity on Campus"
5. Mark Earley, "Faith on Campus," *Breakpoint*, August 9, 2005 (This commentary first aired on December 2, 2004).

Chapter 8: Teach Your Children

1. Acts 16:30-34.
2. Andrea Billups, "Home Schoolers No. 1 on College-entrance Test," *The Washington Times,*" August 22, 2000. Accessed from www.ordination.org/homeschool.htm March 24, 2007.
3. Exodus 13:8b (NLT).
4. Dr. G. Kevin Steger, "Perpetuating the Faith," *Proclaim*, September, 2005, Vol.23, No.9, 6.

Chapter 9: Sin is Crouching at the Door!

1. John 10:10a.
2. Matthew 24:10-13.
3. "Study: Rising number of kids exposed to online porn, and most say it turns them off" *USA Today*, February 5, 2007.

4. Romans 6:23a.
5. James Patterson and Peter Kim, *The Day America Told the Truth: What People Really Believe About Everything That Really Matters*. As quoted in "Truth & Dare," *Acquire The Fire*, Volume 1, Issue 3, pg 10.
6. Genesis 3:1-4.

Chapter 11: The Danger of Air Conditioning Hell

1. Matthew 7:13.
2. 1 Peter 4:18.
3. Jerry Adler, "In Search of the Spiritual," *Newsweek*, September 5, 2005, 48-49. As quoted in McDowell, *The Last Christian Generation*, 34.
4. Kenneth L. Woodward, "Why We Need Hell, Too," *Newsweek*, August 12, 2002.
5. Isaiah 53:5.
6. Hebrews 9:22.
7. "Hell Air-Conditioned," *New Oxford Review 58* (June 1998): 4. As quoted in Christopher W. Morgan & Robert A. Peterson, eds., *Hell Under Fire* (Grand Rapids, Michigan: Zondervan, 2004), R. Albert Mohler, Jr., "Modern Theology: The Disappearance of Hell," 41.

Chapter 14: Rediscovering the Power of Prayer

1. Matthew 6:10b.
2. 1 Samuel 12:23.

Chapter 15: Heroes of Prayer

1. Genesis 19:16.
2. Daniel 9:23 & 10:2-3.

Chapter 16: Prayer That Won't Let Go!

1. James 4:2-3 (NKJV).
2. Luke 9:40-42.
3. Hebrews 11:7a.

Chapter 18: Gospel Lite

1. John F. MacArthur, Jr., *Ashamed of the Gospel: When the Church Becomes Like the World* (Wheaton, Illinois: Crossway Books, 1993), 47.
2. Ibid.
3. Ibid.
4. "Hell's Sober Comeback," *U.S. News and World Report* (March 25, 1991), 56. As quoted in Mohler, Jr., "Modern Theology," 18-19.
5. Mark 16:15 (NKJV).
6. MacArthur, Jr., *Ashamed of the Gospel.*
7. Matthew 5:13-15, Ephesians 4:11-12, 2 Corinthians 5:17-6:1.
8. 2 Corinthians 3:2.

Chapter 19: The Message That Never Loses its Relevance

1. I would like to give credit to Ray Comfort and his message *Hell's Best Kept Secret* for helping me see this truth.

Chapter 20: No Fear!

1. Psalm 111:10, Proverbs 1:7.
2. Proverbs 16:6, Proverbs 22:4, Deuteronomy 6:2.
3. Proverbs 14:26.

4. Charles H. Spurgeon, "The Resurrection of the Dead," a sermon preached February 17, 1856 at New Park Street Chapel, Southwark (London: Passmore and Alabaster, 1857),104. As quoted in Mohler, Jr., "Modern Theology," 28.

Chapter 21: His Mercy Endures to all Generations

1. Luke 19:10.
2. Sherwood Eddy, *Pathfinders of the World Missionary Crusade* (New York: Abindgon-Cokesbury, 1945), 34. As quoted in Ruth A. Tucker, *From Jerusalem to Irian Jaya* (Grand Rapids, Michigan: Zondervan, 1983), 167.
3. Ecclesiastes 3:11.
4. Nahum 3:1.

Chapter 22: Finding the Lost Sheep

1. Ezekiel 34:1-2a.
2. Ezekiel 34:10-12,16.

Chapter 23: Jesus, the Good Shepherd

1. Isaiah 50:6.
2. Isaiah 52:14.
3. 2 Corinthians 2:16.
4. Ezekiel 37:3.
5. Ibid.
6. Ezekiel 37:4-6 (NKJV).
7. Ezekiel 37:9 (NKJV).
8. Ezekiel 37:11.

Chapter 24: Signs of Life

1. Philippians 2:15.
2. John 9:4.

Names of students have been changed throughout the text.

How Many Saviors?

Companion Booklet

Ken speaks directly to the heart of the *Millennial Generation*, and helps them stand against the tide of anti-Christian culture. He deals with the issues they face head on and helps them fall in love with Jesus and become true life-long disciples. Order a copy for the young person you love, or for the whole youth group!

Visit us online at *SoulofaGeneration.com* today to find other resources and tools to reach the Millennial Generation!

Proclaim Magazine

Free one year subscription to *Proclaim*, Ken Dornhecker's monthly ministry magazine. Not only can you keep up with Ken's ministry, every issue is packed with inspiration and information on reaching people for Jesus Christ!

To order your subscription of *Proclaim* or
For speaking engagements

Contact:
Ken Dornhecker
Evangelism Fellowship
P O Box 1915
Burleson, TX 76097

Web site: www.EvangelismFellowship.org
Email: Ken@EvangelismFellowship.org

Printed in the United States
85281LV00004B/130-174/A

9 781602 667297